60 0331642 4

TELEPEN

UNIVERSITY OF NOTTINGHAM

WITHDRAWN

FROM THE LIBRARY

D1348592

MACMILLAN MODERN NOVELISTS

General Editor: Norman Page

MACMILLAN MODERN NOVELISTS

Published titles

ALBERT CAMUS Philip Thody
FYODOR DOSTOEVSKY Peter Conradi
E. M. FORSTER Norman Page
WILLIAM GOLDING James Gindin
GRAHAM GREENE Neil McEwan
HENRY JAMES Alan Bellringer
DORIS LESSING Ruth Whittaker
MARCEL PROUST Philip Thody
SIX WOMEN NOVELISTS Merryn Williams
JOHN UPDIKE Judie Newman
EVELYN WAUGH Jacqueline McDonnell
H. G. WELLS Michael Draper

Forthcoming titles

JOSEPH CONRAD Owen Knowles
WILLIAM FAULKNER David Dowling
F. SCOTT FITZGERALD John S. Whitley
GUSTAVE FLAUBERT David Roe
JOHN FOWLES Simon Gatrell
JAMES JOYCE Richard Brown
D. H. LAWRENCE G. M. Hyde
MALCOLM LOWRY Tony Bareham
GEORGE ORWELL Valerie Meyers
BARBARA PYM Michael Cotsell
MURIEL SPARK Norman Page
GERTRUDE STEIN Shirley Neuman
VIRGINIA WOOLF Edward Bishop

MACMILLAN MODERN NOVELISTS
FYODOR DOSTOEVSKY

Peter Conradi

NOTTINGHAM UNIVERSITY LIBRARY

MACMILLAN

© Peter Conradi 1988

All rights reserved. No reproduction, copy or transmission
of this publication may be made without written permission.

No paragraph of this publication may be reproduced, copied,
or transmitted save with written permission or in accordance
with the provisions of the Copyright Act 1956 (as amended).

Any person who does any unauthorised act in relation to
this publication may be liable to criminal prosecution and
civil claims for damages.

First published 1988

Published by
Higher and Further Education Division
MACMILLAN PUBLISHERS LTD
Houndmills, Basingstoke, Hampshire RG21 2XS
and London
Companies and representatives
throughout the world

Typeset by Wessex Typesetters
(Division of The Eastern Press Ltd)
Frome, Somerset

Printed in Hong Kong

British Library Cataloguing in Publication Data
Conradi, Peter
Fyoder Dostoevsky.—(Modern Novelists).
1. Fiction in Russian. Dostoevskii, F.M.—
Critical studies
I. Title   II. Series
891.73'3
ISBN 0-333-40762-8
ISBN 0-333-40763-6 Pbk

331642

For Jim O'Neill

Contents

Contents

General Editor's Preface

The death of the novel has often been announced, and part of the secret of its obstinate vitality must be its capacity for growth, adaptation, self-renewal and even self-transformation: like some vigorous organism in a speeded-up Darwinian ecosystem, it adapts itself quickly to a changing world. War and revolution, economic crisis and social change, radically new ideologies such as Marxism and Freudianism, have made this century unprecedented in human history in the speed and extent of change, but the novel has shown an extraordinary capacity to find new forms and techniques and to accommodate new ideas and conceptions of human nature and human experience, and even to take up new positions on the nature of fiction itself.

In the generations immediately preceding and following 1914, the novel underwent a radical redefinition of its nature and possibilities. The present series of monographs is devoted to the novelists who created the modern novel and to those who, in their turn, either continued and extended, or reacted against and rejected, the traditions established during that period of intense exploration and experiment. It includes a number of those who lived and wrote in the nineteenth century but whose innovative contribution to the art of fiction makes it impossible to ignore them in any account of the origins of the modern novel; it also includes the so-called 'modernists' and those who in the mid and later twentieth century have emerged as outstanding practitioners of this genre. The scope is, inevitably, international; not only, in the migratory and exile-haunted world of our century, do writers refuse to heed national frontiers – 'English' literature lays claims to Conrad the Pole, Henry James the American, and Joyce the Irishman – but

geniuses such as Flaubert, Dostoevsky and Kafka have had an
influence on the fiction of many nations.

Each volume in the series is intended to provide an
introduction to the fiction of the writer concerned, both for
those approaching him or her for the first time and for those
who are already familiar with some parts of the achievement in
question and now wish to place it in the context of the total
oeuvre. Although essential information relating to the writer's
life and times is given, usually in an opening chapter, the
approach is primarily critical and the emphasis is not upon
'background' or generalisations but upon close examination of
important texts. Where an author is notably prolific, major
texts have been selected for detailed attention but an attempt
has also been made to convey, more summarily, a sense of the
nature and quality of the author's work as a whole. Those who
want to read further will find suggestions in the select
bibliography included in each volume. Many novelists are, of
course, not only novelists but also poets, essayists, biographers,
dramatists, travel writers and so forth; many have practised
shorter forms of fiction; and many have written letters or kept
diaries that constitute a significant part of their literary output.
A brief study cannot hope to deal with all these in detail, but
where the shorter fiction and the non-fictional writings, public
and private, have an important relationship to the novels, some
space has been devoted to them.

NORMAN PAGE

Preface and Acknowledgements

This study is aimed at the general reader and the student of Dostoevsky alike. It sets out to describe his four great novels, and two lesser ones, in simple terms, and to relate them to the post-Romantic debates of the day and to Dostoevsky's 'modernity'. Given this brief, and so short a space in which to fulfil it, it would be hard to do more than sum up a few aspects of the work. In so far as I attempt more, it is to look at the question of Dostoevsky as a *comic* novelist. On the whole it has been other novelists who have noticed how funny Dostoevsky is. Where critics have tackled the comedy, they have tended to relegate it either to 'light relief'; or to 'dark comedy' and the absurd, both by now mid-century platitudes. Ronald Hingley, who last addressed Dostoevsky as a comic writer, wrote that, 'at the elbow of Dostoevsky the devout, there usually stood Dostoevsky the irreverent joker with his water-pistol, sneezing-powder and stink bomb' (1962, p. 217). Well, perhaps. But this suggests that the comic and the serious must stand at odds. My case would be that the comedy is sometimes at odds with the message, but not always. Comedy and message can assist one another, on occasions.

And this is the case, without the work necessarily turning into 'dark comedy' either. The mid-century saw Dostoevsky taken over by a pop-existentialism, for which 'dark comedy' represented an important value. Existentialism, which claimed Dostoevsky as a forebear, and was 'apparently so pitiless and so searching', was in fact the 'opiate of the sub-intelligentsia' and the 'prop upon which the common reader interested in ideas can cheerfully recline'.[1] The importance of 'dark comedy' for the general existentialist viewpoint was that it aligned Dostoevsky with a variety of metaphysical complaint. This is certainly there in his work, but as one element only. Dostoevsky has been used to feed that metaphysical self-pity which has for so long marked one kind of contemporary 'thinker', constituting his deepest piety and his natural intellectual home.

I should like to acknowledge the help of friends, colleagues and students at Kingston Polytechnic. Sarah Johnston and Gail Cunningham made many valuable suggestions. So did Priscilla Martin. Madeleine Evans in the library at Kingston, and Professor Malcolm Jones of Nottingham University, were generous in their help with bibliography. Professor Jones also most kindly and illuminatingly answered queries about the Russian texts. Julie Campbell helped with the proofs. I owe much to delegates of the Sixth International Dostoevsky Symposium held at the University of Nottingham in August 1986. My deepest debt – I hope apparent throughout – is to previous Dostoevsky critics, especially British and American.

References to Dostoevsky's novels are by the divisions of the text (part, chapter, etc.), rather than page, since readers may use widely differing texts. For *The Double*, references are by chapter (e.g. 'ch. 1', in parenthetical references); for *Notes from Underground*, by chapter and section (e.g. '1.1'); for *Crime and Punishment* and *The Idiot*, by part and chapter (e.g. 'I.1'); for *The Devils*, by part, chapter and section (e.g. 'I.1.1'); and, for *The Brothers Karamazov*, by book (*not* part) and chapter (e.g. 'I.1'). My own quotations use the wording of the Penguin editions, and I am grateful to Penguin Books for permission to quote from Dostoevsky's *The Idiot* tr. David Magarshack (Penguin Classics, 1955), copyright David Magarshack, 1955; *Crime and Punishment* tr. David Magarshack (Penguin Classics, 1966), copyright David Magarshack, 1966; *Notes from Underground*; *The Double* tr. Jessie Coulson (Penguin Classics, 1972), copyright Jessie Coulson, 1972; *The Brothers Karamazov* tr. David Magarshack (Penguin Classics, 1958), copyright David Magarshack, 1958; and *The Devils* tr. David Magarshack (Penguin Classics, 1953; repr. with appendix 1971), copyright David Magarshack, 1971. References to Dostoevsky's other writings (letters and diary) are to the editions mentioned in the bibliography.

References to secondary sources listed in the bibliography

are, so far as possible, made parenthetically within the text, by name of author (if not already given) and date. Page references are cited where appropriate.

Chronology

Dates according to the old Russian calendar.

30 October 1821	Dostoevsky born at Mariinsky Hospital, near Moscow, where his father is a surgeon.
27 February 1837	Death of his mother.
May 1837	Goes to military engineering College in St Petersburg with his brother Michael.
June 1839	His father dies, probably murdered by his own serfs.
May 1845	Belinsky enthusiastic about *Poor Folk*.
February 1846	*The Double* published.
April 1847	Dostoevsky starts to frequent the Petrashevsky circle.
23 April 1849	He is arrested.
22 December 1849	Mock execution in Semonovsky Square. Sentence commuted to four years in prison and four years as a private in the Siberian army.
6 February 1857	Marries the widow Maria Dmitrievna Isaeva.
26 March 1858	Released from army service.
1861–2	*The House of the Dead* published.
1862–5	Makes three trips abroad.
1864	*Notes from Underground* published.
15 April 1864	First wife dies.
1866	*Crime and Punishment* published. Anna Snitkina engaged as stenographer. Dostoevsky dictates *The Gambler* to her. They become engaged.
1867	Second marriage (to Anna).

1867–71	They live abroad.
1868	Publication of *The Idiot* starts.
1871	Publication of *The Devils* (also translated as *The Possessed*).
8 June 1880	Dostoevsky makes his 'Pushkin speech' in Moscow.
November 1880	Completes *The Brothers Karamazov*.
28 January 1881	Dostoevsky dies.

1
Introduction

About three days before the publication, in *Crime and Punishment*, of the description of Raskolnikov's murder of the old pawnbroker and her sister, the Russian papers carried a news item of a nearly identical murder. Dostoevsky was pleased at his own artistic foresight. By the end of his career it had become commonplace to describe Dostoevsky as a prophet, and the 'prophetic' description has never died. Twentieth-century critics habitually write of the ways in which he appears to have understood, or even forecast, our century as much as his own. Indeed, celebration of his genius in the West has sometimes taken on the character of a metaphysical rant, as if the dance of ideas in his work existed outside history. The prophetic claim is still in no danger of being understated. As with the philosopher Nietzsche, with whose name Dostoevsky's has often been linked, it is not uncommon to read that it is 'even now too early fully to understand what he had to tell us' (Lord, 1970, p. xi); while C. M. Woodhouse tells us that those wishing to know how the world will feel in the year 2020 should read the maddest pages of *The Devils* (1951, p. 107). How does he know? And what does it mean to assert this? Dostoevsky is sometimes described as if he were a twentieth-century novelist *manqué*, born, by a freak of chance, too early: a strange compliment since it flatters us as much as it does him.

The American critic Joseph Frank, to whose massive biography of Dostoevsky this chapter is greatly indebted, has recently provided one useful corrective. He has shown how rooted all Dostoevsky's thinking is in the tumultuous intellectual debates of his day; while E. H. Carr earlier provided a rebuke to exaggerated claims by arguing that Dostoevsky was a better psychologist than philosopher, suggesting not merely how sheepish the great writer was in each phase of his political

1

views – following, rather than creating, intellectual fashion – but also how hare-brained on occasion. The author of *The Brothers Karamazov*, which champions universal brotherhood, argued also that 'war is health-giving and eases humanity' (Carr, 1931, p. 275), and was also hostile to Jews, Germans, the French, Catholics and Poles – among others – and befriended the dislikable Pobedonostsev. Pobedonostsev was a high priest of reaction and the ideological policeman of the late Tsarist years, tutor to Tsars Alexander III and Nicholas II and lay head of the Orthodox Church, instigating mass murders of Jews. Yet Pobedonostsev provided Dostoevsky with one source for the Grand Inquisitor in *The Brothers Karamazov*. It is, to say the least, an equivocal portrait.

There is a clear gap, in other words, between Dostoevsky the artist and Dostoevsky the man. It is the first and most important of the many 'dualisms' in his character, a split that results in the extraordinary sense of freedom the reader experiences, and in a freedom of interpretation that may be called recognisably modern. Indeed, Dostoevsky's novels seem 'modern' and 'relevant' in a way that is true of no other single nineteenth-century writer: what other work by a writer of his time retains the same power to shock and move us? Or to make us laugh? Dickens, perhaps, and even his genius looks oddly *cosy* by the side of the darker Russian who loved his work. Lafcadio Hearn warned a century ago about the possibility that *Crime and Punishment* might drive its readers mad (see Wasiolek, 1962, p. 32). That book still retains, in a way that seems to me true of no other novel of its time – unless it be other Dostoevsky novels – the power to keep the reader awake at night, so distressing and disturbing is it. Moreover, this is a power that transcends ideological borders. In 1971 Russian crowds queued through the night to enter their names on a subscription list for the new Soviet Academy edition of their beloved author's writings (J. Jones, 1983, p. 4). At the very end of his life he was to praise Pushkin both as the great national poet and as an international writer, in his 'Pushkin speech'. The same is true of Dostoevsky. The most passionately Russian of writers, he has been adopted by many other cultures as their own. There is an 'English' Dostoevsky, with which this study will be partly concerned, a 'German', a 'French' and an 'American' Dostoevsky. Can the influence of any other nineteenth-century

writer be discerned in as wide and international a company of
writers as Faulkner, Dreiser, Mann, Kafka, Gide, Malraux,
Camus, Iris Murdoch and Angus Wilson?

Dostoevsky's claim to be a 'modern' as well as a nineteenth-
century writer has many sides to it. Nietzsche, Freud and the
existentialists have all been happy to enlist him as a forebear;
the least tamable of great writers, critics have fought over his
reputation and he has been claimed for wholly opposite belief-
systems, Christian and nihilist, reactionary and socialist. The
world of his novels is giddy and disordered, unstable rather
than stable. His tales take place in a zone of spiritual crisis and
incipient social anarchy that speaks directly to our condition.
So does the fact that his characters are solipsists, imprisoned in
windowless, private worlds which they have constructed
themselves. Raskolnikov in *Crime and Punishment* and Stavrogin
in *The Devils* take their solipsism to a demonic pitch, undertaking
to live 'beyond morality'. The moral anarchism for which they
speak fascinated and haunted Dostoevsky, and each of his four
great novels centres around or culminates in a murder, and is
in part a psychological thriller and Gothic romance. The Gothic
novel has a plot based on murder, suspense and mystery. It
puts its characters into situations of extreme erotic or
psychological tension, and tends to an atmosphere suggestive of
the supernatural or the demonic. It has often been derogated to
the status of mere 'entertainment'. Many considerable writers –
Dickens, for example, mix it with other modes. Dostoevsky is,
surely, the greatest of all writers of modern Gothic, and rare in
his single-minded exploration of the genre. Today, when many
talented writers reject a narrowly conceived social realism in
favour of a new Gothic – among them Angela Carter, Ian
McEwan, Iris Murdoch, Martin Amis and Beryl Bainbridge –
Dostoevsky's fantastic realism points the way.

Moreover, he combines all this with comedy. It is a comedy
of an extraordinary and 'modern' sort. He combines tragedy
and farce with an (apparent) callousness. The deaths of the
Marmeladovs in *Crime and Punishment* are both deeply harrowing
and wildly comical. He may initially have learnt this tone of
comic grotesquerie from Gogol and from Dickens. In what he
does with it he goes further than either. In his mature fiction we
are exposed to real pain and simultaneously defied not to laugh.
This comedy is not, I believe, 'incidental' or decorative, it is no

mere emollient to draw the sting of our reaction or provide
'light relief'. Instead it can be used to intensify our response to
the horrors he has to describe and complicate our judgement of
the action. His use of comedy will provide a major theme in the
present study.

Perhaps his use of comedy is one reason why Dostoevsky, the
most idea-bitten if not the most ideological of novelists, is also
the most open-ended to read. There is a grim comedy in the
way his characters are hounded by ideas, and through this
comedy Dostoevsky undercuts his own moral passions, tests
and purges his own ideals.

A related way in which he opens up his own texts is through
exploring the 'doubleness' of his own creations. He is the
greatest writer to have addressed himself so wholeheartedly to
the theme of the 'double', of man's psychological and ethical
self-alienation. Bakhtin noticed (1984, *passim*) how Dostoevsky
deprives the reader of any reassuring 'official' spokesperson for
his own views. Even his good characters – Myshkin in *The Idiot*,
Alyosha in *The Brothers Karamazov* – are free from being simply
his mouthpiece. And this is, in part, because his are among the
first fictional characters to be clearly in the grip of their own
unconscious selves. His first major work, as we now read his
career, was *The Double*; and, in teaching us about the doubleness
of his own characters, and in lending them much of his own
radical insecurity, he educates us too about our own.

To look at this instability and doubleness, and at Dostoevsky's
ability to focus contradictory emotion, it may help to outline
some of the doubleness and contradiction his own tragi-comic
life contained, as young progressive and older reactionary, as
devout believer and tormented sceptic; and as a man capable
both of great folly and also of fearless and remorseless self-
analysis.

*   *   *

Fyodor Mikhailovich Dostoevsky was born on 11 October 1821.
He is the only major Russian writer of his time not to have
been born into the landed gentry – as Pushkin, Lermontov,
Gogol, Turgenev and Tolstoi all were. In later life he was to
criticise 'landowner's literature' for its false and pastoral calm
(Mochulsky, 1967, p. 497). Where more patrician writers such

as Tolstoi found order, inherited values and calm, he found instability, disturbance, breakdown.

He was the second son of Dr Dostoevsky, who worked in a military hospital. The Dostoevskys claimed descent from a sixteenth-century family of Lithuanian nobles, since fallen on hard times and sunk to the despised caste of non-monastic clergy. Despite Russia's rigid social hierarchy, Dostoevsky's father succeeded in rising from the priestly caste in which he was first trained to that of civil servant. Gaining admittance to the Imperial Medical Surgery in 1809, from 1829 he worked at the Mariinsky Hospital for the Poor, outside Moscow. In 1828 he was enabled, through promotion, to inscribe himself on the rolls of hereditary nobility, and, in 1831–2, when Dostoevsky was ten, his father bought two small estates 150 versts (about 100 miles) outside Moscow. The strong sense of social aspiration together with keeping-up-appearances reminds the English-speaking reader of Dickens's family background. The Dostoevskys thought of themselves as 'old gentry' but had in fact climbed back into the new service nobility created by Peter the Great. They had a small, cramped, crowded apartment near the hospital. Space was always a problem; and money often. His mother came of merchant stock, richer than the Dostoevskys but lowlier in status. His mother's sister had married into another rich merchant family, the Kumanins, with whom the Dostoevskys had, over half a century, uneasy relations. The Dostoevskys borrowed money from the Kumanins but resented them.

A long tradition associates Dostoevsky's father with the Karamazov father in *The Brothers Karamazov*. In fact, so far from being a dissolute old cynic, he was hard-working and was sufficiently valued at work to be offered a large promotion to postpone his retirement. He was, however, a man of explosive temper, violent and strange, rigid, depressive, mistrustful, and with a suspicious and morbid sensitivity that his second son partly inherited, as he did his quarrelsomeness, irritability and hypochondria. Devoted to his wife to a pitch of pathological jealousy, he tended to dramatise his life and its failures, seeing himself as a righteous man persecuted like Job, and justifying both his extreme egocentricity and his own weakness in the grandest terms. Few writers, once more apart from Dickens, portray so many unhappy, neglected and pauperised children

in their work, or so few adequate parents. It is hard to know
how much of the family chaos that rules Dostoevsky's fictions
one should read back into his early life. His father appears to
have taken the paternal role conscientiously. He did not beat
his children, and Dostoevsky was later to call his parents
'outstanding people' (Frank, 1977, p. 18). He met Fyodor's
demands for money and encouraged the children to study and
read. Yet relations between them were not good. The five
children appear to have been terrified of their father's strange
temper. The four months a year they spent alone with their
mother at Darovoe in the country must have been a happy
escape. They lived there in a small thatched three-room cottage
sheltered by lime trees and could play unsupervised. The few
happy childhoods depicted in Dostoevsky's work take place in
the country. His mother, Marya Fedorovna, was warm, cheerful,
compassionate and loving. As late as 1925 the legend of her
kind heart and leniency survived among the Darovoe peasants.

Some incidents from this time throw light on later
preoccupations. With the housemaid Vera at Darovoe the
children one day entered the chapel and, taking down the
icons, made a mock-religious procession through the fields, a
sacrilege they repeated. The idea of sacrilege seems to fascinate
the adult Dostoevsky: in *The Brothers Karamazov* Smerdyakov as
a child hanged cats and buried them with mock-religious
ceremony. The children also met a *durochka* or female half-wit
called Agrafena, who was raped, made pregnant and lost her
child. She may have been one prototype for Lizaveta in *The
Brothers Karamazov* and for Marya Lebyatkin in *The Devils*. In
1833 fire destroyed much of the family's country property,
including many of the peasant huts. Alyona Frolovna, the
Moscow townswoman who acted as housekeeper-*cum*-nanny,
and who shared much of the piety of the serf class, offered all
her savings to Madame Dostoevsky. This touched and impressed
the young Fyodor, as did an incident when he was out in the
fields and became terrified by a cry he thought he had heard of
a wolf on the loose. A *muzhik* (peasant) named Marey, who was
ploughing, comforted the distraught child, making the sign of
the cross and sending him safely home. This latter incident
loomed large in Dostoevsky's later idealisation of the peasantry.

Children from more patrician homes often encountered the
Russian Orthodox faith, as indeed they learnt the Russian

language, only after they had absorbed both free-thinking and French. Dostoevsky was from the start steeped in his native language and the Gospels. He was later to say that the problem of the existence of God had haunted him all his life. He was unable to conceive of a world that bore no relation to God, but unable, either, wholeheartedly to believe. From his mother he inherited her superstitious piety and generous sensibility. She died from consumption in 1836, the year in which Dr Dostoevsky had his two eldest children admitted to the Academy of Engineers in St Petersburg. Fyodor was already at that age committed to literature, recording as much distress over Pushkin's death as over his mother's. The profession of military engineer was at odds with his deepest instincts. But in 1838 he and Andrey left for the Academy.

The murder of his father by his serfs in June 1839 was the most important event of his youth. Freud, in a famous essay,[2] makes it the pivotal event of Dostoevsky's entire life. Dostoevsky had not seen his father for two years. He was in St Petersburg, while his father had retired owing to ill-health to Darovoe. Now isolated, he had gone to pieces. He drank heavily and was overheard having long conversations with his dead wife. He took his misery out on his peasants. And he slept with one of his housemaids, who bore him a child.

Joseph Frank shows that the rumour that his peasants sexually mutilated him remains a rumour only. Recent Soviet scholarship, moreover, has cast doubt on whether the death of Dr Dostoevsky was a murder at all: the story of a murder *may* have been invented by a neighbour involved in a lawsuit with Dr Dostoevsky, anxious to secure the dead man's estate after his peasants had been deported to Siberia for their 'crime' (Frank, 1977, p. 86). What is certain is that Dostoevsky *believed* that his father had been murdered by his serfs; and he may have felt implicated. He had incurred debts as a student and made frequent requests to his father for cash, all of which were eventually met. A fellow student, Count Semenov, judged the young Dostoevsky extravagant by comparison with himself and put down his requests for (among other things) new boots, tea and a trunk, to his desire to emulate wealthier comrades, a desire testifying to the young Dostoevsky's deep insecurity. As Frank says, 'He was exploiting his father's meagre resources to appease his craving for social status' (p. 87). The news of Fyodor's

failure to achieve promotion had already helped cause Dr
Dostoevsky to have a small stroke. Fyodor may well have
surmised, therefore, that his father's cruelty to his peasants,
which had presumably goaded them to this extremity, had been
exacerbated by his own thoughtless extravagance.

Freud saw Dostoevsky as caught between a guilty Oedipal
desire to murder his own father – a desire whose actualisation
(as he supposed) roused his guilt to an overwhelming pitch –
and a consequent desire to identify with that very father-
principle he had so sacrilegiously challenged, and thus organise
his own punishment. Freud's suggestion that Dostoevsky's
epilepsy was brought on by news of his father's death and was
a hysterical symptom of the intolerable tension set up between
two irreconcilable desires is altogether more questionable.
Recent scholarship suggests that his first seizure may not have
occurred until much later, and was by no means 'hysterical'.
The death of Dostoevsky's three-year-old son Aleksey from a
severe epileptic fit in 1878 suggests a hereditary origin for the
disease. None the less, Freud's reading of Dostoevsky's life as a
psychodrama of rebellion against 'authority', and at the same
time identification with it, is brilliant and rightly influential.
Dostoevsky's greatest work, *The Brothers Karamazov*, concerns
the attack on two aspects of authority – God and the father,
atheism and parricide. Such a division of energy between
challenge to power and reconciliation with it undoubtedly
colours Dostoevsky's relations both with God and with the
'Little Father', the Tsar, and powers the major novels. He
questioned Nicholas I's regime, and supported Alexander II's.
Freud's analysis of this major duality or split in Dostoevsky-as-
artist is deservedly a famous one.

In a letter to his brother about his grief at his father's death,
Dostoevsky goes on to say that the aim of his life henceforth
will be to study 'the meaning of life and man. . . . Man is an
enigma, this enigma must be solved, and if you spend all your
life at it, don't say you have wasted your time, I occupy myself
with this enigma because I wish to be a man' (*Letters*, 16
August 1839).

*   *   *

Before pursuing the story of Dostoevsky's career, a word about the Russia of the 1840s is necessary. Russia's triumph over Napoleon in 1812 had brought Russians into contact with the comparative freedom of Western Europe, and led to the hope that Tsar Alexander I would institute reforms. The disappointment of these hopes led, in 1825, to the rebellion of a few aristocratic insurrectionists against the newly crowned Tsar Nicholas I, who condemned five of the 'Decembrists', as they came to be known, to death, and the remaining thirty-one to be exiled for life in Siberia. Nicholas I's 'barrack-room regime' froze all Russia into a terrified immobility, which only the massive defeat of the Russian army at Sevastopol in the Crimean War of 1854–6 served to disturb. Nicholas I died not long after. Entry into the vast and strictly graduated civil service established under Peter the Great, and advancement within it, became national obsessions; toadyism and inefficiency the inevitable by-products. A third of the 60 million Russians were serfs, the relic of a late feudalism whereby the tenure of land was considered in terms of the peasants on it who paid tax to their landlord. Any threat to this stultified system was regarded as seditious. Nicholas's Minister of Education stopped all university courses in philosophy and metaphysics, and transferred the teaching of logic and of psychology to theology departments. Nicholas, himself a monstrous anachronism, *personally* vetted the writings of, for example, Mikhail Lermontov, both before and after that writer's exile to the Caucasus for sedition, just as he supervised the sacking of schoolmasters whose pupils slouched in class. The intelligentsia, in such a system, were marginal. Their special alienation looks forward to, and speaks directly to, the estrangement of many twentieth-century readers today. It might indeed be said that the Russian intelligentsia *invented* 'alienation'; and the 'superfluous man' who carried its special burden of futility, figures throughout the century, from Lermontov's *A Hero of Our Time* (1840), through Goncharov's *Oblomov* (1859), to Turgenev's *The Diary of a Superfluous Man* (1850) and *Rudin* (1856), and Chekhov's *Uncle Vanya* (1897).

Gogol's *Dead Souls* (1842) satirises the moral squalor and inertia of this Russia. A swindler buys up the title to serfs who have recently died and then mortgages these titles before the deeds can be revised. His journeyings through provincial Russia reveal a rogues' gallery of incompetence and triviality.

Dostoevsky read Gogol enthusiastically and could quote him by heart. He was a passionate reader all his life. His enthusiasms at this time were for Romantic idealism and Romantic radicalism, and his reading-list fed both: Scott, Mrs Radcliffe, Schiller, Pushkin, George Sand, Balzac, Hugo, E. T. Hoffmann, Shakespeare and Racine. He early translated a novel by Sand, and then Balzac's *Eugénie Grandet*.

Although he was born a Muscovite, we associate him with St Petersburg. He is that city's greatest chronicler. 'The most fantastic city with the most fantastic history of all the cities on earth', he called it (*Winter Notes*, ch. 3). Compared to Moscow, St Petersburg was the symbol of Russia's desire to absorb Western progress and rationalism. Yet it was also a potent symbol of the cost of that desire. Its building by Peter the Great in the early eighteenth century, out of a wilderness of Finnish marsh, had cost the lives of many hundreds of serfs; and it was also the nerve-centre of state tyranny, with its giant chancelleries and its humiliated and terrified *chinovniks* (clerks) who populate the short stories both of Gogol and the young Dostoevsky, and who seem to look forward to Kafka's haunted clerks in our century. The vast, impersonal, fantastic city, the brains and heart of the vigorous, expanding Russian Empire, its sense of unreality, its insufferable summers, 'white nights' and winter fogs – all these, rather than the city's beauty, haunt Dostoevsky's fiction.

On his and his brother's way to St Petersburg occurred an incident Dostoevsky was never to forget. At a posting-station the boys watched a government courier beat the young peasant driver of his troika on the back of the neck with his fists, and then saw the driver frantically whipping up his horses. Nearly three decades later, in the notebooks for *Crime and Punishment*, Dostoevsky noted to himself, 'My first personal insult, the horse, the courier.' And in January 1876 wrote that this sickening picture had stayed with him all his life (*The Diary of a Writer*). As a young man he interpreted the vices of the Russian peasantry entirely in political terms: they fed his radical fervour. Later, they were to be subsumed into the mysteries of God's relation to man, and of the existence of evil, pain and suffering.

Dostoevsky's first important work, *Poor Folk*, is set in St Petersburg and owes something to Gogol, to whom it alludes and whom it rebukes. In a society in which all organised opposition is forbidden, literature becomes the sole available political weapon. *Poor Folk* is a sentimental novel written in the form of letters, concerning the failed love-affair between a poor elderly copying-clerk, Makar Devushkin, and a dishonoured girl, Varvara Dobroselova. Devushkin reduces himself to yet more abject poverty in buying gifts for Varvara, and, loving the girl, suffers on her behalf. Finally her seducer shows up and marries her solely to create an heir and dispossess a nephew. The novel brought a wholly new insight and respect to the endless humiliations of poverty. Devushkin's goodness carries with it an implied promise of universal brotherhood, a promise cruelly denied by a harsh regime. Dostoevsky said of his generation of writers that 'We all came out from under Gogol's overcoat', a sentence that implies both debt and distance.[3] In Gogol's famous story 'The Overcoat', the hero, Akaky Akakievich, has his life transformed and his fragile sense of identity vouchsafed by the acquisition of a cheap overcoat, which is then stolen. An Important Person to whom he turns for help insults Akaky, and, in a fantastic coda, he returns to haunt the Important Person. Akaky has no developed inner life, and the stand-point from which the story is told is infinitely superior to that of the clerk, who is affectionately mocked as well as pitied. Devushkin complains that Gogol has written a hostile and insulting caricature.

Grigorovich and Nekrassov were so moved by *Poor Folk* that they awoke the young Dostoevsky at four in the morning to tell him so. And the great radical critic Belinsky, an influential arbiter, was next day equally enthusiastic. It is hard today to recapture Belinsky's excitement, which depended, in part, on his having found an ally in the fight to create a Russian social realism. The later novels eclipse *Poor Folk*'s sentimental optimism. Dostoevsky's friend Maikov acutely suggested that Varvara may secretly feel far more guiltily oppressed by the very generosity of her benefactor Devushkin than by her crushing poverty. This is exactly the kind of uncomfortable perception that the later fiction brings home to us. In *Poor Folk* it is understated.

Dostoevsky was none the less lionised by Belinsky and his *Pléiade* circle, and courted by Turgenev. When this acclaim was tempered by doubt over his next works, Dostoevsky showed himself at less than his best. He seems to have been maddened by his sudden fame to a pitch of boundless self-glorification and over-excitement – few of his emotions then knew much sense of proportion – and maddened therefore to an equal pitch by his subsequent rejection. It was a rejection in which he colluded, through an unrealistic politics of confrontation with the *literati*. His enmity with Turgenev was to mark his life. Nekrassov's mistress reports him at this stage as nervous, impressionable, easily unnerved, pathologically shy and self-conscious. Eager to impress and conquer, he was also highly strung, spoiling for fights he could not cope with. Belinsky wrote of him that Dostoevsky was convinced that all mankind envied and persecuted him. His brilliance at depicting states of hysterical suspicion, persecution and tormented sensitivity had its roots in his own psyche.

After his estrangement from the Belinsky circle he found companionship among the set surrounding Mikhail Butashevich-Petrashevsky, a twenty-six-year-old much influenced by the new ideas – especially Fourierism – coming from France. For Fourier, society repressed the individual, and economic competition caused wars and poverty. The expression of passion would lead to harmony, and a new order could be created and run by 'phalansteries' – self-sufficient, mainly agricultural units of production resembling luxury hotels and producing fantastic wealth – whose inhabitants would practise free love and enjoy gigantic French meals. Fourier was an amiable and tolerant utopian anarchist, rather than a puritanical communist. In his later recoil from the ideas of utopian socialism, Dostoevsky was to use Fourierism, in *Notes from Underground*, and again in *Crime and Punishment*, as a butt for satire.

The Petrashevtsy – as the group came to be known – comprised a number of conflicting groups and interests. Dostoevsky belonged to the Palm-Durov group, whose musical–literary character was used as a screen by the glamorous, hot-headed leader of the activists, Speshnev, in whose debt Dostoevsky reported himself after a while to be, and who was later to sit as one model for Stavrogin in *The Devils*. The degree of Dostoevsky's complicity with Speshnev's secret inner group is still unclear: the authorities luckily never found it out. It was the institution of serfdom that Dostoevsky principally hated, rather than the autocracy. A police spy, Antonelli, tried to monitor the meetings of the Petrashevtsy, and, in the early hours of 23 April 1849, the secret police arrested Dostoevsky, and some sixty others. His apartment was searched and his papers confiscated. He was never to complete *Netotchka Nezvanova*, which he was in the middle of writing. Solitary confinement in the Peter and Paul fortress followed. There were grotesque rather than terrifying interrogations. He fought against nightmares, nervous disorders, piles, and behaved with dignity and courage. By 17 September, twenty-three of the Petrashevtsy were charged with crimes, and seventeen of these, including Dostoevsky, condemned to execution by firing-squad.

They were not told of this sentence in advance. Neither were they told that the Tsar planned to stage a last-minute scene of mercy in which their sentences would be commuted to hard labour; he enjoyed acting the role of all-powerful, all-merciful ruler. Dostoevsky thus lived out the unimaginable drama, and the grisly black farce, of believing himself minutes away from certain death, and then of enjoying a miraculous reprieve. They were taken to a snowy Semenovsky Square, where, despite the pleasures of seeing one another again after half a year's solitary confinement, they noticed a twenty-to-thirty foot platform hung about with black crape, with some stakes to one side. Sentence to death by firing-squad was read out to each man – this took half an hour – and they were given long peasant blouses as shrouds. A priest with Bible and cross summoned them to repent. The first three men were tied to the stakes, their caps pulled over their faces – though Petrashevsky defiantly kept his uncovered – before an aide-de-camp galloped onto the scene carrying the real sentences. One of the prisoners had meanwhile gone mad, and never recovered. They were now given convict head-gear, soiled sheepskin coats and boots. Within two days they were *en route* for Siberia and hard labour, with ten-pound shackles on their feet.

Dostoevsky was never to forget what it had been like, standing there, in terror of death, awaiting execution. Twenty years later he gave his favourite hero, Myshkin in *The Idiot*, both a passionate indictment of capital punishment, and, later in the same novel, a description of what he had felt:

It seemed to him then that he had only five more minutes to live ... those five minutes were like an eternity to him, riches beyond the dreams of avarice; he felt that during those five minutes he would live through so many lives that it was quite unnecessary for him to think of the last moment, so that he had plenty of time to make all sorts of arrangements: he calculated the exact time he needed to take leave of his comrades, and decided that he could do that in two minutes, then he would spend another two minutes in thinking of himself for the last time, and, finally, one minute for a last look around. . . . He was dying at twenty-seven, a strong and healthy man; taking leave of his comrades he remembered asking one of them quite an irrelevant question and being very interested indeed in his answer. Then, after he had bidden farewell to his comrades, came the two minutes he had set aside for thinking of himself; he knew beforehand what he would think about: he just wanted to imagine, as vividly and as quickly as possible, how it could be that now, at this moment, he was there and alive and in three minutes he would merely be *something* – someone or something – but what? And where? All that he thought he would be able to decide in those two minutes! There was a church not far off, its gilt roof shining in the bright sunshine. He remembered staring with an awful intensity at that roof and the sunbeams flashing from it. He could not tear his eyes off those rays of light: those rays seemed to him to be his new nature, and he felt that in three minutes he would somehow merge with them. . . . The uncertainty and the feeling of disgust with that new thing which was bound to come any minute were dreadful; but he said that the thing that was most unbearable to him was the constant thought, 'What if I had not had to die! What if I could return to life – oh, what an eternity! And all that would be mine! I should turn every minute into an age, I should lose nothing, I should count every minute separately and waste none!' (1.5)

'Life is gift, life is happiness, every minute can be an eternity of happiness', he wrote in a buoyant letter later the same day to his brother Mikhail. His terrible experience seemed to trigger in him a passionate sense of the unconditional authority of the Christian commandment to love and to forgive. It was he who consoled the stricken Mikhail, when the time came for them to part.

Wives of the Decembrists at Tobolsk, who were waiting

twenty-five years to return to European Russia, gave the convicts food, clothing and comfort. Their devoted self-sacrifice made a deep impression on Dostoevsky, and he treasured the New Testament they gave him, reading it on the day of his death.

The experience of a decade in Siberia, which now followed, seems neatly to divide Dostoevsky's career as a thinker into early radicalism and later conservatism, as belief in a political cure for Russia's ills gave way to a preoccupation with a spiritual or religious solution. Indeed, Dostoevsky's life has sometimes been turned into a parable to exemplify the message of the four great novels that he wrote on return from Siberia, which put a high value on redemptive suffering. According to this view, Dostoevsky's life-story or life-myth embodied the wisdom he preached: seduced by Belinsky into atheism and socialism, he paid bitterly for his intellectual crimes before rediscovering Christ through the Russian people.

The truth, as Frank has demonstrated (1977, p. 254), is of course more complex. The young Dostoevsky would lose control of himself when the hardships of the peasants were mentioned; the older Dostoevsky made a cult of the people into an article of superstitious faith. He certainly moved from political revolt towards a more reverential acceptance of God's world, but his early radicalism was based on no theoretical opposition to autocratic rule, properly managed. And his later 'Russian socialism' – in which he was, of course, now one of the new generation of radicals' bitterest opponents – shared none the less with his early thinking an advocacy of the social institutions of the Russian peasantry, including the *artel* (workers' wage-sharing co-operative) and *obshchina* (communal ownership of land). As for his religious feelings, these, despite moments of inspiration, were throughout his life subject to anguished questioning and uncertainty. So far from being seduced into atheism by Belinsky, he was disturbed to the point of tears when, in 1847, Belinsky attacked Christ. To many of the utopian socialists of the 1830s, Christ was the first social revolutionary; and Dostoevsky's Christianity after 1860 still retained a strongly humanitarian flavour.

Yet the Siberian years did mark a change of direction. One puzzle about them concerns Dostoevsky's experiences with the convicts he now met. The later Dostoevsky was to make a cult of the Russian people nearly religious in its intensity. Yet his great fiction contains few portraits of 'the people', apart from convicts, thieves and murderers. Tolstoi and Turgenev persuade us that they know the Russian peasantry better. Dostoevsky essentially belonged to the half-Europeanised intelligentsia created by Peter the Great, which was severely alienated from the Russian poor. He came to believe that a reconversion of his own class to the values of the people would effect a cure for this split. The disease at least was real enough.

Among the first shocks of the camp at Omsk was meeting real depravity: male and female prostitution, thievery, drunkenness. In 'An Honest Thief' Dostoevsky had written of a pauper who died of remorse after stealing the breeches of an equally destitute friend, to buy some vodka. The *real* convicts, however, displayed no such pretty sentiments. Although he later idealised the brotherhood he found with ordinary convicts, what he actually encountered was unrelenting class hatred. The idea that the peasants might have accepted gentry leadership in their efforts to find freedom was a delusion. Petrov, in the famous bath scene in *The House of the Dead* – the book which commemorates Dostoevsky's years at Omsk – fussed tenderly over the author but coolly stole his Bible, none the less. The convicts' abuse of, and hatred and contempt for, the political prisoners poisoned much of his time there.

If the gain to his political thinking is questionable, the experience undoubtedly enriched the creative artist, in plumbing the depths of human irrationality, cruelty and evil. He met Orlov, who had murdered children and old people in cold blood; Orlov died running the gauntlet. Aristov had cynically betrayed seventy innocent people to the infamous Third Section (the secret police) for cash and then lived riotously on the proceeds; while in Ali the sweet-tempered Tartar Dostoevsky met gentle goodness. But the encounter with men who lived beyond ordinary moral inhibition gave thrust to that fascinated vision of moral anarchism that his great novels seek to defend themselves against. Dostoevsky may have been flogged at the orders of the terrible Major Krivtsov, the camp commandant, a petty barbarian and drunk; he seems also now to have suffered his first epileptic seizure, an experience that he described in *The Idiot* as possessed of an ecstatic mystical aura, despite the convulsions and the fear of death or disability. He read and enjoyed Dickens's *Pickwick Papers* and *David Copperfield*.

When he left the camp he wrote to his benefactress, Madame Fonvizina,

> I will tell you that I am a child of the century, a child of disbelief and doubt . . . and will remain so until the grave. How much terrible torture this thirst for faith has cost me and costs me even now. . . . And yet, God sends me sometimes instants when I am completely calm . . . and it is at these instants that I have shaped for myself a *Credo* where everything is clear and sacred for me. This *Credo* is very simple, here it is: to believe that nothing is more beautiful, profound, sympathetic, reasonable, manly and more perfect than Christ . . . if someone proved to me that Christ is outside the truth, and that *in reality* the truth were outside of Christ, then I should prefer to remain with Christ rather than with the truth. (*Letters*, 20 February 1854)

This remarkable assertion has been used to argue both for the persistence of Dostoevsky's religious faith and for its perversity. In reality, Dostoevsky needed Christ as an ethical ideal. It was with God the Father rather than the Son that he felt the need to struggle.

He had four more years to serve in exile, as a private in a line battalion in Semipalatinsk, and, from 1856, as an officer. Siberia at this date shared something with the American West: a pioneer mentality, stockaded outposts, a policy of colonisation and shifting alliances between the European Russians and the many Asiatic tribes who formed raiding parties. In this wilderness Dostoevsky fought his way back into Russian letters, campaigning for the right to publish once more. He also fell hopelessly in love, with Marya Dimitievna Isaev, who was married to a one-time schoolmaster and customs officer, a drunkard whose alcoholism rendered his family destitute. He and his wife probably played a part in Dostoevsky's creation of the Marmeladovs in *Crime and Punishment*. She was a pretty thirty-year-old blonde who had consumption and was given to quixotic outbursts of violent indignation against life's injustices. Isaev died and, after other suitors were seen off, she and

Dostoevsky married. It was probably on her side a marriage of convenience, while he had been starved for so long of female company that his feelings for her had a quality of desperation; their melodramatic intensity was equalled only, so far as we can tell, by the unhappiness the relationship caused him. Unlike his second wife, but like Dostoevsky, Isaeva was not a person of strong emotional balance. She died in 1864, a few years after he had re-established himself in Petersburg. She left a wastrel son by her first marriage, Paul, whom Dostoevsky loyally supported.

In addition to his struggle to re-enter the literary scene, there were struggles over money, and a number of tussles over love. In the early 1860s Dostoevsky and his brother were involved in editing two unsuccessful magazines – *Vremya* and *Epocha*. The first provided a forum for his *The House of the Dead* and for *The Insulted and the Injured*; the second took the start of *Notes from Underground*, his most famous short novel. Imperial decree suppressed *Vremya*. *Epocha* failed financially. *Vremya* had published the short story of a young student, Polina Suslova, with whom Dostoevsky corresponded, travelled and fell in love. It was she who showed him 'how intimately hate may be interwoven with love. She had revealed to him the appetite for cruelty and . . . for suffering, the sadistic and masochistic, as alternating manifestations of the sexual impulse' (Carr, 1931, p. 112). Dostoevsky's fiction displays no happy sexual relationships, and he knew much about self-humiliation and self-degradation in both their 'spiritual' and also their more earthly passionate guises. He wrote of the affair in his hastily composed novella *The Gambler*.

Until his second wife put his affairs into some sort of order, Dostoevsky was an unremittingly irresponsible businessman, who needed debts in order to write and who left his writing-commissions until the last possible moment. He was rarely out of debt. A generous giver, he was also a frequent borrower. The 1860s was the decade of his gambling-mania, of visits to the tables at Wiesbaden and Baden-Baden, and of the repeated cycle of short-term gain leading to catastrophic loss, followed by abject self-abasement. The pawning of his winter overcoat more than once marked the coming of spring. At this time he entered into a potentially disastrous contract. The publisher Stellovsky paid him 3000 rubles for the right to issue a collected edition of his writings, to include one novel that was to be delivered by 1 November 1866. Among the penal provisions for late delivery was an infamous clause granting Stellovsky the right to publish all of Dostoevsky's writings, past and future, without further payment, should this new novel be more than one month late.

Dostoevsky signed. By September 1866 he had written not one word of the promised novel. In the past he had avoided the debtor's prison by assuring his creditors that there would disappear their last hope of reclaiming their money. The sequel, fantastic as it is, belongs to one of his own fictions. Three friends first proposed to 'ghost' the promised novel, and then came up with the further suggestion that he dictate it *viva voce* to a stenographer. And this he did. On 3 October, Anna Grigorievna Snitkina, aged only twenty, arrived at his flat to start dictation of what was to be *The Gambler*. On 30 October they delivered the finished novel of 40,000 words, written in twenty-six days. On 8 November Dostoevsky proposed marriage to Anna and was accepted.

The years that follow are those both of his greatest literary success and of his domestic happiness. Anna was a simple, determined young woman, detested by Dostoevsky's relatives, to a number of whom he was indiscriminately but faithfully generous. Her mixture of girlish worship and maternal solicitude seems to have suited them both. Partly to save him from the relatives who were living off him – Paul Isaev, Dostoevsky's drunkard brother Nicholas, and his brother Mikhail's widow – and partly to win him entirely for herself, Anna took him abroad for four years. She weaned him slowly off his gambling-obsession, and was canny enough not to cramp his style at the tables, but to give him enough rope repeatedly to hang himself with. When they returned to Petersburg in 1871 they owned only the contents of their travelling-trunks. Everything else had been forfeited to their creditors or sold by their relatives. But Anna took his business affairs in hand, herself publishing *The Devils*, a sensational popular success, in book form, and for forty years continuing to publish his work.

The new security 'told' in terms of his artistic maturity. These are the years of his great works: *Crime and Punishment* (1866), *The Idiot* (1868), *The Devils* (1879) and finally *The Brothers Karamazov* (1880). We see Dostoevsky in the role of passionate spouse and comically anxious *paterfamilias*, desolate

at the loss of a child, being consoled by the midwife during his
anguish at the birth of another, visiting Bad Ems in Germany
to cure his lung trouble, fussing amiably and helplessly when
separated from his wife. After the many years of torment and
uncertainty, the years of bourgeois respectability sat strangely
on his shoulders. He addressed the world through his monthly
Diary of a Writer and assumed the prophetic mantle referred to
earlier. He took great pains to answer the many letters from
admirers that dogged his last days. In dealing with fame as he
did, he oddly recalls Tennyson, like whom he was often a
victim of his own moods; and in both writers there was a great
simplicity and want of guile.

He was still under police surveillance, his mail being opened,
until shortly before his death. This came suddenly, on 28
January 1881. He suffered a haemorrhage in his lung, and after
three days asked for the New Testament given him by the
Decembrist wives on his passage to Siberia in 1849. The words
he found on opening it – 'And Jesus answering said unto him,
Suffer me now for thus it becometh us to fulfil all righteousness',
from the Gospel according to St Matthew – seemed to him a
token of his approaching end. So rapid was his decline that
Anna's brother, arriving unawares from Moscow, was amazed
to be accosted by an undertaker who told him 'some writer'
had died – 'I forget the name'. Dostoevsky died at the zenith of
his fame. Some 30,000 people attended the funeral in the
Church of the Alexander Nevsky Monastery. There were
seventy-four wreaths, and so many speeches that, some six
hours after the funeral service had begun, the crowds around
the grave had not yet begun to disperse.

2

The Double (1846) and *Notes from Underground* (1864)

If *Poor Folk* concerned the pains of want of status and money, *The Double* is about the pains of identity itself. Dostoevsky did not, of course, invent the theme of doubleness. It haunts nineteenth-century literature, from E. T. Hoffmann's tales – for example, 'The Devil's Elixirs' – to R. L. Stevenson's *Dr Jekyll and Mr Hyde*. Dostoevsky had read Hoffmann, where the theme is treated as lurid melodrama and associated with 'animal magnetism'. His immediate source, however, was Gogol's heartlessly whimsical and funny stories 'The Nose' and 'Diary of a Madman'. In the latter a poor clerk and quill-sharpener, Poprishkin, falls in love with the daughter of his office chief, and goes mad when she is wholly unregarding. He decides he is the King of Spain, and his asylum a court. In 'The Nose' the Collegiate Assessor Kovalyov's nose plays truant, and goes about town in the uniform of a more exalted rank, taking carriages and praying in the cathedral, before returning to its owner as mysteriously as it first departed. Ambition in a stagnant society has no sane outlet, seems to be the message. *The Double* combines the themes of the splitting of one person (as in 'The Nose') and of ambition punished by madness (as in 'The Diary of a Madman'). While it also takes Hoffmann's psychic melodrama and flattens this into a banality as oppressive as Gogol's, the extended psychological treatment is pure Dostoevsky. We have seen that, in Dostoevsky's life at this time, acute shyness, self-disgust and paranoia were not unknown: literature here affords a further splitting and doubling of the author's persona, as his characters mimic and duplicate him (see Mochulsky, 1971, p. 54).

The Double, in Dostoevsky's revised and abbreviated 1866

version, has thirteen chapters. At the start, Titular Councillor
Golyadkin wakes from deep sleep in his dingy room unsure if
he is still dreaming. The mood is one of bizarre animism: his
carefully itemised belongings, which vouchsafe his sense of
himself, all familiarly return his gaze. The dull autumn day
peers into the room with a sour grimace. His room and the day
tell him he is at home on Shestilavochny Street. Yet his
surroundings are not inert but uncannily alive. Even the
samovar gabbles and lisps its invitation to be put to use. And
his mirror informs him that he is sleepy, short-sighted, balding,
insignificant, but *all right*.

He is excited about what the day holds in store. He gloats
over his money, and his cheekily insubordinate servant
Petrushka arrives in an inconceivably odd costume: bare-foot,
yet in a hand-me-down suit with tarnished gold braid made for
someone a whole foot taller, with a hat and scabbarded sword.
Travelling in a blue hackney-carriage with a heraldic device on
it and Petrushka outside, Golyadkin shrinks into a corner on
sighting some fellow clerks, who point at him and seem to call
his name impolitely. He puts them down as 'young cubs', 'just
trash'. Then he sees Andrey Phillippovich, his head of section,
staring at him. Golyadkin blushes in great confusion and blurts
out an explanation: 'It's quite all right; this is not me at all,
Andrey Philippovich, it's not me at all, not me, and that's all
about it' (ch. 1). This absurd clowning sets the stage for the
moment when he will indeed appear as his own double, himself
but also not himself. It also prepares us for a quality not
merely of Golyadkin's but of the narration through which he is
presented. As John Jones excellently puts this (1983, p. 78),
'the novel is as mad as its hero'. It mocks the critic's attempt to
find safe ground among its dippy inconsequence. Having
proferred this bizarre 'explanation' of the pomp in which he is
travelling, Golyadkin directs a terrible challenging stare at the
carriage corner into which he had previously shrunk, a stare
designed to defeat his enemies. This is a tale full of staring and
glaring. He then feels an immediate need to 'say something
very interesting to his doctor'.

In chapter 2, with Dr Rutenspitz, Golyadkin is divided
between solecism, apology and defiance. He cringes, hectors,
practises his special challenging stare. Rutenspitz advises him
to change his habits, warning him against solitude. To this

Golyadkin replies, 'I am a man apart'. Golyadkin is always on the verge of being offended, stumbling in acute self-consciousness. He decries the fashionable world he is decked out to enter, where people make puns and do 'clever tricks'. His manner is pompous, his tone one of self-proclamation and whining self-justification, in which each statement affords a ghostly echo or backwash of meaning that is the opposite of what is actually said. 'I am a little man – but not sorry to be a little man; I am proud not to be a great man but a little man. I am not an intriguer, and proud of that too.' He protests too much: we have already witnessed both his resentment at his inferiority and his bizarre desire to assert himself. His claim not to think himself intrinsically insignificant is hollow. He decries the wearing of masks, another theme of the tale; Golyadkin refers on four occasions to those who need masks.

Goli, in Russian, means naked, and Golyadkin proceeds to unmask himself unwittingly as just such an intriguer as he decries. After further bluster and some tears he reveals two rankling obsessions. His boss's nephew Vladimir Semyonovich has been promoted at work to the rank of Assessor. He has, moreover, been courting the same girl as Golyadkin has set his heart upon – Clara Olsufyevna. Golyadkin has both congratulated 'our darling boy', as he satirically calls him, in a distinctly malicious manner, and also warned Clara Olsufyevna against the nephew's 'mixed motives'. He further claims that both nephew and uncle have injured him by spreading rumours about his having basely and insincerely offered his hand to a German cook to avoid paying her what he owed her for food. His recurrent sensitivity about this, through the tale, suggests that he fears it is partly true.

Throughout this confession he refers to himself not directly but with elaborate obliquity as 'This person I know very well'. For the purposes of supposed discretion, he disassociates himself from himself, a mistrust that comes to a head when he abruptly leaves the doctor, murmuring that he now understands him completely, dismissing him for a fool.

In chapter 3, Golyadkin shops. Of course, this is no ordinary shopping. Posing as a rich man, Golyadkin bargains for a complete tea and dinner service, and gets an elaborate cigar-case and silver shaving-equipment thrown in. He undertakes to call for these items next morning – 'or even that day', but without vouchsafing the worried shopkeeper any deposit. The word 'even', in 'even that day', comes straight out of Gogol. It proposes a logic for the fictional world according to which one course of activity might be thought more unreasonable than another, when in fact the whole tale is weightless and causeless. The word 'even' mocks the everyday expectations it summons up and cannot satisfy.

Golyadkin is restless, unable to eat or concentrate on the newspapers. Another encounter with his two fellow clerks leaves him wounded. His strange bombast and self-advertisement merely amuse them: 'Up till now you have known only one side of me.' He is working himself up to the necessary pitch to go to his beloved Clara's dinner-party, where the footman refuses him, telling him that Olsufi Ivanovich is at home, 'Or rather no, sir, he's not at home.' Another double! And one that mocks the convention that private and public selves may be thought of as separate. Olsufi Ivanovich is in the house but chooses not to receive Golyadkin. Was Golyadkin even invited? We never learn.

He has further snubs to undergo. Gerasimych the old butler politely but rmly refuses him, and meeting his boss Andrey Phillippovich he once more justifies himself: 'This is my private life'. Like so many of the poor clerks that haunt Russian literature, he is pleading for a fragile sense of identity, asking that his personal display shall not prejudice him at work. At the same time the story suggests that private life in Golyadkin's sense scarcely exists in Petersburg. The youth who was promoted was also the youth deemed to 'deserve' Clara, and in deserving Clara perhaps also merited promotion. In both respects he is unlike Golyadkin, who is making a feeble protest at the rigid scheme of things, as the sub-title, 'A Petersburg Poem', suggests. Golyadkin's speech never suggests that he possesses a strongly individual, private world: he does not so much talk as *speechify*, and his talk is full of declamation, stale truism and cliché. The small inner world he does possess, in his unconsciousness, is now about to escape him in any case, and become fully visible.

Chapter 4 concerns the social gathering from which Golyadkin is, for the moment only, excluded. The tone is one of arch and elaborate burlesque. The narrator is full of mirth at his incapacity to rise to the occasion, rhetorically speaking, or describe its many glittering 'virtues'. He nicely makes clear both how third-rate the participants are – given to bribery and nepotism – and simultaneously 'places' Golyadkin's tormented desire to be received there. The effect is to isolate Golyadkin, not merely from the party, but also from the complicity between narrator and reader, so that his absolute exclusion invites our pity and horror more than our sympathy.

Meanwhile, in a rubbish-filled, dark, cold back-passage, Golyadkin is waiting for three hours to gatecrash the party, musing and berating himself for his purported cowardice and base behaviour. Bumping into a number of guests on the way, and tearing one old lady's dress in his hurry, he pushes his way into Clara's presence. Blushing and getting flustered, nearly dumb and blind in his self-conscious extremity, his odd behaviour brings the room to complete silence. After repeating his assertion to his boss that his visit is unofficial, he retreats into a corner where the proximity of a tall and handsome youth with a devastating smile makes him feel like 'an utter insect'. When his attempts to make himself feel at home through talking are snubbed, he keeps silent. He indulges romantic fantasies of saving Clara, for example from a falling chandelier, when Gerasimych once more advances to throw him out. Golyadkin, after some bluster, clumsily approaches Clara to dance with her. She screams, and the crowd separates them, after which he is propelled out into the cold.

This must be accounted one of the first of Dostoevsky's *skandal* or fiasco scenes, in which a group, usually a large one, is disrupted and brought to a pitch of shameful disorder by the untoward actions of one of its members: a device he later developed to great dramatic and structural effect.

It is also after this scandalous public scene, in which all his premonitions of public shame and insult are at last fully met, that Golyadkin meets his double. He is twice described in chapter 5 as 'beside himself'. The metaphor comes to life, at the point of maximum humiliation and self-alienation, as he *literally* materialises his estranged deeper psyche at his side. There are further images of horrified disassociation – it was as if he were 'trying to hide from himself, as if he wanted to run away from himself'. And then he sees someone, like him bundled in clothes from head to foot, prancing, trotting, with small pattering steps like his, and, again like him, with a small hop in his gait. Almost shrieking aloud, he stops dead, his hair standing on end: nearly insensible from horror, he has recognised himself.

The remainder of the tale concerns the success of this new Golyadkin, Golyadkin Junior – poaching on and invading many of the enterprises where Golyadkin Senior had met with failure. His upward career is to coincide with Golyadkin Senior's downward one and final madness.

The following morning Golyadkin is divided between hope that he may have imagined it all, and dread that it is *at the office* that something is wrong. In a tone mixing farce and melodrama he thinks he might fall ill and die as a pretext for not going to work: 'The death-rate's very high, especially just now.' His alignment of his own case with the statistical norm bespeaks both the fragility and the obstinacy of his sense of self; his ominous sense that work is the source of his malaise points a similar moral.

Golyadkin Junior is indeed at the office, acting meek and bashful but oddly at ease. Golyadkin experiences a nightmarish shame and horror. As with the blankly sinister yet oddly taken-for-granted world of Kafka's fiction, Golyadkin's fellow clerks express not the smallest surprise at Junior's arrival. One colleague politely assures Golyadkin that the same thing happened to an aunt of his: she saw her double just before she died, and he adds some banal speculations about nature's bounty and Siamese twins. The two Golyadkins accompany one another home. Junior's first name, his patronymic, his very hat and coat, all exactly resemble Senior's.

Still aping polite embarrassment and pretending to self-effacement, Junior tells his life-story, a commonplace tale of losing a post in the provinces, of humiliation and poverty in Petersburg until he found his new position in Senior's department. Disarmed and taken off guard, Senior launches into a series of absurd, inconsequential yet revealing anecdotes, through which he shows off his general knowledge and pretends to a worldly self-command. Junior writes him a quatrain of rare fatuity, thanking him for advice, hospitality and patronage, which prompts Senior to invite him to move in with him, and to swear eternal love.

The following morning, not merely has Junior disappeared without warning, but *so has his bed*. The Golyadkins' encounter is the first in a long series in which Junior, becoming each time more devilishly insolent, betrays a moment of intimacy with Senior. At work Junior not merely now affects scarcely to recognise his 'benefactor' but addresses him in 'officialese'. Junior has won a moral victory, and the scales of power have tipped in his direction. From now on little impedes his progress. It is as if Junior represented a *successful* version of the *persona* Senior had adopted when he tried to better himself socially, and through his engagement. Junior now prances, minces, bustles and skips with self-importance. He cheats Senior out of a document he had been copying, and steals the honour of completing it himself. Junior's rise is to be Senior's fall. Like Grishka Otrepyev, a mountebank who challenged Boris Godunov over the Russian throne in the seventeenth century, Junior is usurping Senior's place and identity.

In chapter 9 Senior berates himself: 'How do you feel now? . . . Will you do something now, you scoundrel, you rogue?' Junior is the apparent rogue. So Senior's remark is odd, until we absorb the fact that Junior is acting out his own unconscious wishes. Musing at a restaurant, he finds himself presented with a bill for eleven savoury patties, ten of which have been devoured by Junior, who left him to pick up the bill. Junior appears, reposing in his new sense of power. Senior weeps from hurt pride. He writes Junior a letter associating his appearance with his enemies, accusing him of stealing his papers and his good name. The letter is stupid with respectable indignation. It is taken by the now drunk and fractious Petrushka. 'Good people live honestly', says Petrushka. 'They never come in twos.' But the letter is intercepted by Regional Secretary Vakhrameyev, who replies with abuse. Golyadkin waxes sententious, moralising about those who 'know their place'. An ironic phrase: Senior began the tale with ambition, and the thwarting of this ambition bred his 'double'. To know one's place means to stay an integrated, or at least a single, personality. Not to know it means to be duplicated. Senior dreams that Junior is supplanting him, and moreover is telling the world that it is he, Senior, who is the counterfeit, a dream that ends with an endless stream of replicas of himself springing up from each step he takes, each revolting in its depravity.

Indeed, Junior does replace Senior at work, and Senior is now received there coldly. A public scene is staged in which

Junior, very much at home, embraces his colleagues and includes Senior by accident. He then drops Senior's hand with disgust as if he had touched something filthy, and mocks him by shouting, 'Give us a kiss darling' – an allusion to the German fiancée. Junior is now a court-favourite with the dignitaries, swollen with excited self-importance, yet socially skilful as Senior never was. In another interview between them Senior pleads, idiotically, that his letter about Junior's depravity should be taken *in exactly the opposite sense* from that in which it was written; but, on departing, Junior repeats the gadfly gesture of the morning, as if Senior's hand were unclean.

Senior is now deserted by everyone. A message instructs him to give up his work to Ivan Semyonovich. Petrushka leaves him for the German woman. He sermonises to Petrushka with a florid unreality: 'There is a sadness lurking even in gilded palaces. . . . Before every man lie many different roads.'

The last chapters see him awaiting his beloved Clara Olsufyevna, from whom he has mysteriously received a romantic letter asking him to elope and save her from another suitor. In the last chapter, awaiting her behind a woodpile after yet another twitting by his double, he bizarrely mixes up self-hatred with desire for revenge on her bid for independence (if that is what it is: the 'reality' of her letter to him is impossible to prove). She deserves a whipping, he decides, for her romantic ideas. He is discovered in his hiding-place, where 'masses of people . . . a flower-show of ladies' descend on him in a mood of general pathos. Junior, however, despite impersonating contrition for his gloating malevolence, at the last moment reveals an 'unseemly and sinister joy' as Senior is handed over to Rutenspitz and the lunatic asylum. 'Our hero shrieked and clutched at his head. Alas! This was what he had known for a long time would happen.' So ends the story.

*   *   *

Richard Peace has shown how belief in the monistic (single) nature of man was a central doctrine of Russian radical thought, and in 1859 Dobrolyubov was to claim that 'dualism' had been disposed of long ago. It was the despised liberals who equivocated about radical reform and who displayed ambivalence. *The Double*, despite having been written during Dostoevsky's 'radical' period, is inhospitable to the spirit of radicalism, and Belinsky was unenthusiastic about it. Chernyshevsky was later to present human behaviour in his epochal *What is to be Done?* as 'straightforward, clear-cut and rational'.[4]

There is little that is straightforward about *The Double*. Its insistent lack of surface realism vexes interpretation. Is Golyadkin Junior 'real' or a 'projection'? A world in which your work-fellows instantly accept your dividing into two is not an accountable one in the ordinary sense. The novel is, moreover, full of such quizzical touches: the bed that disappears after Junior has slept in it, the letter from Vakhrameyev into which some brand-new points get introduced – or clarified – overnight (ch. 10); the appearance of the strange letter from Clara suddenly inviting Golyadkin to elope; the money (750 rubles) inexplicably in Golyadkin's possession at the start: the story is indeed as mad as Golyadkin himself.

This is not to deny a 'political' reading. The story can be read as showing that a pathological self-subordination denies man the luxury of an integrated personality; and that a society that requires such subordination is a wrong one. Junior acts out Senior's unconscious wishes, and it is his function also to punish Senior for having those wishes. He represents Golyadkin's desires, and also the penalty that 'society' exacts for these aspirations. Junior acts out the roles of toady, gossip and hypocrite that Senior is unaware of within himself; but he gets away with it, and his success paradoxically enforces the timidity and hypocrisy by which 'society' is internalised within Senior as a voice of conscience. This is doubtless so, but leaves out of account all that makes the story profoundly unsettling. A tyrannical social order can crush and maim personality, but Dostoevsky seems to hint at the doubleness and the sickness of *all* personality.

Dostoevsky recognised that the tale is not a complete success, but also insisted on the significance of its major idea. He referred to Golyadkin as 'my supreme Underground Man' (J. Jones, 1983, p. 56). The link with the great story of the 1860s is instructive. Both *The Double* and *Notes from Underground* are anatomies of unreason. Both attack a rationalist soul-picture. Both insist that man's nature is not unitary, and, as a concomitant, that the lower half is at war with the higher. Both look forward to the major fiction, in which the characters are so often at war with themselves, and in which Dostoevsky's self-divided personalities confront either their real doubles (Ivan talking with Smerdyakov in *The Brothers Karamazov*, for example) or their hallucinatory doubles (Ivan having a waking nightmare of meeting the Devil, in the same novel).

In *Notes from Underground*, however, Junior's spiteful manipulation of Senior turns into the Underground Man's spiteful manipulation of the reader himself. Similarly, the 'voluptuous satisfaction' that Golyadkin hints that he gets from masochistically hurting himself becomes not merely one item in the psychological decor, but an essential and subversive part of the foreground.

It is in this work that the significance of Dostoevsky's continuing polemic about doubleness begins to become clearer. Walter Kaufmann called *Notes from Underground* 'one of the most revolutionary and original works of world literature' (1956, p. 14), a judgement echoed when Lionel Trilling wrote of its challenge to the entire tradition of European humanism. As for its narrative strategy, John Bayley has suggested that it opened up a path from which all twentieth-century writers have profited.[5]

The book was written during a time of both personal and social crisis. Dostoevsky's first wife Masha was dying in an adjoining room; and there were, as so often, dire financial troubles. Besides bearing the traces of his private anguish, the book is Dostoevsky's first important entry into the cultural debate of the 1860s, in which Chernyshevsky's *What is to be Done?* figured so importantly. To follow the rhetoric of *Notes from Underground*, some account of this contemporary debate is essential.

The 1840s and 1860s represent the most notable epochs in the history of nineteenth-century Russian radical thought. Dostoevsky's apprentice fiction was written in the 1840s, and the period of his mature fiction, after his ten-year exile, began in the 1860s. The hatred between radicals of these two periods – the word is not too strong – figures in many contemporary works. It is an estrangement movingly portrayed by Turgenev in his masterpiece *Fathers and Sons* (1862), which annoyed both parties. In it the supercilious dandy Pavel Petrovich, a man of the 1840s who never travels without his portable bath and silver dressing-case, fights a duel with the young nihilist doctor

Bazarov, who respects no authority except that of science. Turgenev's real interest, after the generational conflict, was in the unfreezing of their two different styles of masculine egoism, an unfreezing in which love plays a crucial role.

Turgenev was himself, of course, very much a man of the 1840s: that is, a member of the gentry-intelligentsia who dreamt of bringing a Western European humanitarianism to bear on the problems of Russia. The new *raznochintsy* of the 1860s – new men without official rank or status, scions of the clergy, *petit bourgeoisie* and peasantry uprooted through education – held such old-fashioned liberals and their ideas in contempt. They charged these liberals with replacing political activism with a 'cult of the beautiful soul', and with being inert or incompetent before the actual stagnation and backwardness of Russian life. Instead of the weak patrician heroes of Turgenev's fiction, with their mystique of frustration, Chernyshevsky and other *raznochintsy* championed a new 'strong' populist hero. The ferocity of the conflict, into which Tolstoi and Herzen as well as Turgenev were drawn, has no direct equivalent in twentieth-century Anglo-American life.[6] In a country in which all political activity was taboo, 'ideas' were alive in an unusually energetic sense. They arrived in Russia late and untestable, their potency conserved therefore in a singularly pure state, since there was little chance of spending their force in constructive social action.

The debate is opened by Turgenev's *Fathers and Sons* and magisterially closed, as Joseph Frank notes (1983, p. 251) by Dostoevsky's *The Devils* in 1871. There the generations once more collide in the effete 1840-ish dandy Stepan Verkhovensky, and his demonic revolutionary son Peter; but for the first time both generations are indicted equally, and the responsiblity of the older generation in fathering the new is apparent. In between came Chernyshevsky's *What is to be Done?* Its main claim to fame today, apart from being a favourite book of Lenin's, is the savage and direct ripostes Dostoevsky served it in *Notes from Underground* and in *Crime and Punishment*. Chernyshevsky wrote it in the Peter and Paul fortress, awaiting a twenty-year term of hard labour in Siberia that was to break him. Despite one's admiration for his great courage in suffering for his views, it is a very bad book.

What is to be Done? concerns a group of young people. Vera is saved from selling herself to a fop by Lopukhov, who gives up a

medical career for her. She sets up a sewing-shop that becomes
a Fourieresque phalanstery – a co-operative with profits evenly
distributed. She then falls in love with Kirsanov and her
husband disinterestedly commits suicide to clear the way for
their union. The book's philosophical pretensions come from
liberal economists and utilitarians – Adam Smith, Malthus,
Ricardo, and especially J. S. Mill, whom it cites. It propounds
a theory of 'rational egoism' frightening in its forlorn simplicity.
Briefly, man is governed exclusively by self-interest, but because
of this would at once become wise if his true interest were
pointed out to him. 'The wicked will prefer the good as soon as
they can love it without injury to their own interests' (ch. 3,
section 3). This utilitarian philosophy is purportedly born out
by the plot, in which all the main characters are: stout-hearted,
strong and rational, simple and unperplexed. Lopukhov throws
into the gutter a pedestrian who marches straight at him
without turning aside – an episode with a direct echo in *Notes
from Underground*. Kirsanov similarly worsts, in a straight fight,
a nobleman's son who tries to cheat him out of a fee. In the
background is the shadowy, symbolic figure of Rakhmetov, the
revolutionary who sleeps on a bed of nails, eats raw steak and
lives a life that is half-monk's, half-athlete's. The feminism of
the book is moving, and its depiction of the 'new woman', its
striking discussions of prostitution, free love and the new sexual
freedoms, are impressive. Yet Chernyshevsky is so dedicated to
the rational that, like many a revolutionary – and notably
unlike Dostoevsky – he is secretly embarrassed by the erotic, and
none of the protagonists has time for sex itself. It is a mystery
how Vera produces a child, in parenthesis, on the last page.
Finally, all this stalwart belief in the coincidence of true reason
and true selfishness, with Lopukhov's selfless suicide and
Rakhmetov's attempt to 'rationalise' Vera out of her grief, is
underpinned by a bogus mystique of 'science' and the 'scientific'
that is utterly of its time and is embodied here by medicine.
Bazarov in *Fathers and Sons* was a doctor. And *What is to be Done?*
is peopled by doctors and medical students – Lopukhov, Vera,
Kirsanov.

   Notes from Underground revels in the dark Eros eschewed by
Chernyshevsky and has two chapters. The first, in eleven
sections, is philosophical and reflects the debates of the time;
then chapter 2, 'A Story of the Falling Sleet', recounts events

that took place sixteen years earlier, during the 1840s, the period of youthful idealism of both Dostoevsky and his 'anti-hero' (2.10), who remains nameless throughout. In what Leonid Grossman has called some of his most utterly naked pages (1974, p. 310) Dostoevsky focuses his young idealism through older, disenchanted eyes. It is an acutely uncomfortable and distressing book, occasionally a funny one. Its cruel capacity to embarrass its readership remains part of its subversive power.

The Underground Man opens his confession with a proclamation:

> I am a sick man . . . I am an angry man. I am an unattractive man. I think there is something wrong with my liver. But I don't understand the least thing about my illness, and I don't know for certain what part of me is affected. I am not having any treatment for it, and never have had, although I have a great respect for medicine and for doctors. I am besides extremely superstitious, if only in having such respect for medicine. (I am well educated enough not to be superstitious, but superstitious I am.) No, I am refusing treatment out of spite. That is something you will probably not understand. Well, I understand it. I can't of course explain who my spite is directed against in this matter . . . .

The Underground Man at once buttonholes the reader, taking us into his confidence and manipulating our response with agility. The experience of reading resembles being detained by a perverse buffoon who, despite his waywardness and disturbance, gradually, discomfortingly, shows us that his claim to our intimacy is not superficial. John Jones nicely speaks of an 'indecent exposure of consciousness' (1983, p. 263). A short, skinny forty-year-old collegiate assessor, an impressionable orphan and outsider with an inability to meet other people's gaze, he describes himself as 'without character'. A man of the nineteenth century is morally bound to be 'without character', he says, and to lack the stupidity of the strong man who acts. Dostoevsky, through his anti-hero, carefully confounds the categories of 'weak' and 'strong' character that bedevilled contemporary debate. The Underground Man is 'weak' but no idealist; instead he alternatively glories in his powerlessness, with a riotous glee, and, when he can find someone weaker than himself to dominate, glories in his power. He tells us that he was once a sentimental idealist – in the 1840s, when the second half is set. His confessional is an act of revenge on the ideals he once served.

He is another 'superfluous man'; and his initial, chattering proclamation of his 'sickness', which will in any case come to seem as much moral as physical, sets the tone. The 'spite' he cites as an excuse for not seeking medical advice is typical, pointless, hurting only himself. The pleasures of such pointless malice run through the tale and belong in a long list of perverse pleasures that disconfirm the facile moral psychology of Chernyshevsky and the utopian blueprints of the new materialists. The latter argued for a simplified, tidied-up picture of the soul, where good and bad were easily identifiable and good could be simply encouraged through rational exhortation. The Underground Man argues against any such simplified or systematised view of human nature. He uses himself as principal case-study in evidence for the prosecution. The first part is a brilliant, cavalier attack on the new rationalism, from a largely theoretical point-of-view. The second will be a pragmatic verification of the paradoxes asserted in the first.

The pleasure of spiting oneself by refusing medical help is the first in a long series that the Underground Man discusses and acts out. There is the pleasure of confessing, of showing off one's sores in public – inviting shame, achieving shamelessness, as Trilling put it. There is the pleasure of despair, the pleasure of being smeared with filth, the pleasures of self-degradation and debauchery, the pleasure of being hurt and humiliated. Then there is revenge, and the pleasure of building elaborate life-myths and stories around it. Even in howling at one's toothache, the Underground Man tells us (1.4), there is a kind of pleasure. If for 'tooth-ache' we read 'soul-ache', we have a clear picture of the perverse pleasures of the narration itself, in which is buried a cry of pain, too.

The Underground Man's spite – that essential Dostoevskian emotion – destabilises his narrative. He tells us he is a bad civil servant and then claims this is a lie he told 'out of spite' (1.1). The exposure of one lie opens up the possibility that he may now be practising a new one. He invents his emotions – remorse, love, suffering – out of boredom and fear of emptiness. And yet these emotions are real, too. And yet, again, he cannot

? does this indicate unstable reasoning? insensible chatter?

inhabit them with conviction. All thinking, all self-awareness is profoundly unstable. Each piece of reasoning pulls another, 'even more primary, in its wake, and so on *ad infinitum*' (1.5). He enacts the shifting, devious, unending quality of thought, which seeks but also fears a final resting-place. He seeks self-definition through his witty yet carefully unstylish chatter, but eschews it when it approaches. Although he acknowledges a debt to the Romantic confessional of Heine and Rousseau, he seems here to look forward to Samuel Beckett's monologues, and Nabokov's *Lolita*. Might he be called 'lazy'? Laziness might provide him with an identity, even a *career*. He sneers at the respectable hypocrites who praise 'the highest and best' in *theory* while belying their own ideals by living as lazy gluttons. By implication, and by contrast, he praises his own honest doubt and depravity. Thought itself is a form of disease or wound, continually attempting its own unsuccessful cure; each 'cure' inflicts a new hurt or displacement. Thought is 'pointless chatter, a deliberate pouring out of emptiness' (1.5). 'Joking through clenched teeth' he calls his own style (1.9), which none the less suggests that he displays recurrent sources of anxiety.   ? EXISTENTIALISM?

In chapter 1, section 7, the Underground Man addresses the new rationalism. He cites a friend who beautifully and lucidly expounds 'the rational' in any given situation, but always goes on to do the opposite. How can 'rationalism' account for this man? 'All these beautiful systems – these theories of explaining his best interests to man with the idea that in his inevitable striving to attain those interests he will become virtuous and noble – are, in my opinion, nothing but sophistry.' Against any such hygienic ideal he sets 'one's own free and unfettered volition, one's own caprice, however wild, one's own fancy, inflamed sometimes to the point of madness' – 'that is the one best and greatest good'. He attacks the scientific reduction of man, under the guise of utopian philosophising, to a mere cipher, a 'spring on a barrel-organ', or piano-key, stripped of desires, will, volition. As in an old theological paradox, he continually proclaims man's partial free will, even at the price of his willing evil: indeed the capacity of man to will evil becomes, for him, the very sign of his freedom. Freedom to be ungrateful, freedom to be stupid.

Has history, he asks us, anything remotely to do with

RATIONALISM against one's own free volition, one's own caprice and sometimes, wild fancy. and he views scientific reasoning as of no value.

'reason'? In its stale and repetitive violence, its incessant bloodshed, the one thing with which it has no possible connection is *reason*. 'Blood flows in torrents, as merrily as champagne.' Man *thinks* he loves progress. In fact he also loves chaos and destruction. UM ENCOUNTERS A RIVAL AND SEEKS RE

Chapter 2. 'A Story of the Falling Sleet', tests out the Underground Man's alternative soul-picture and shows it to be true. Set in the 1840s, when he was twenty-four, the narrative recounts the offence the Underground Man once took at being pushed idly out of the way by a passing officer. He broods for years about this slight to his vanity, writes a libellous story about the officer that remains unpublished, considers challenging him to a duel after two years in a letter that simultaneously invites his friendship. He buys an imitation raccoon collar in order to have a suitable uniform with which to cannon into the officer on the street and redeem his 'honour'. When he meets the officer, however, he finds himself rolling to one side like a ball. At exactly the point when he has abandoned any further scheme of revenge, he once more finds himself confronted by the officer and, released from prior strategy, is able to barge into the officer 'on an equal footing'.

The paradox of wanting the officer's esteem, yet wishing to fight him to secure it, sets the stage for the main episode, in which the Underground Man tries to manipulate his relationship with his so-called 'friends' Zverkov and his crew, and, later, the prostitute Liza. In a fit of desire to 'embrace all of mankind' he visits Simonov, whose uncertain regard for him holds his interest, and finds that there is to be a farewell dinner for the good-looking, popular, vain Zverkov. He gatecrashes the party, which includes Ferfichkin, a 'nasty, insolent little braggart' (2.3) and Trudolyubov – tall, chilly, honourable and military. He arrives an hour too early, since no one has bothered to let him know that the plans for the dinner have been altered. Feeling snubbed, he provokes Zverkov and then challenges Ferfichkin to a duel. The others ignore him and, for three hours, smiling scornfully, he paces between the table where his friends sit and the stove: the 'nastiest, most comical and most terrible' hours of his life (2.4). Then he begs the others' pardon and is once more snubbed. They are leaving for a brothel, where Zverkov has claimed in advance the favours of Olympia,

* i.e. main episode contained within the story of
the Falling Snow.

U.M. gatecrashes a party, but this party is disbanded when
certain of the friends leave to party at end a brothel.

a girl who, we find, once refused the Underground Man because he had a 'funny face'. UM

He pursues them to the brothel, fantasising alternately a romantic scene of reconciliation in which the others kneel and beg his friendship, and also a scene of confrontation in which he slaps Zverkov's face and challenges him to a duel. They have already left when he arrives there. We next see him (2.6) after he has made love to Liza, a twenty-year-old from Riga. Having got to know her a little, he tries out on her a description of a romantic idyll of family life he claims she is missing. She offends him by seeing through the bookishness of this vision. He then moves on to a picture of her possible brutal death, and neglected funeral in the rain, decking out his word-picture with such touches as the obscene comments of the undertakers. This time the pathos of his account touches her and she weeps and confides further in him. Recognising a certain kinship between them – as will Raskolnikov with the prostitute Sonya – and feeling sorry for her, he leaves his address. i.e. UM GIVES HIS ADDRESS TO LIZA.

There follows one of the blackest and cruellest scenes in modern literature. Having borrowed money to pay back his UM cronies, to whom he writes a lying 'apology', he quarrels with his servant Apollon. Apollon's narcissism, manipulativeness and love of power all echo that of the Underground Man himself. Apollon is his double, and he feels his being 'chemically combined' with his own (2.8). At this point Liza enters, and he feels humiliated by her witnessing the squalor in which he lives and his petty squabbling with Apollon. 'Why did you come? I was laughing at you', he shouts at her. He is trying to pass on to her his own sense of humiliation and powerlessness. 'I say let the world perish, if I can always drink my tea.' In the midst of this furious diatribe against her, against himself and against the world, he notices that she is listening, not to his versatile insults, but to the pain that underlies them. She understands UM and is prepared to love him. Excited, he makes love to her once DOUBTS more; and then, in a final burst of malicious rage, and HER pretending she has come for business purposes rather than out MOTIVE of love, he insults her vilely by paying her five rubles for her AND SINCERITY services. She understandably drops the money and runs away LIZA into the falling sleet. He never sees her again. His soliloquy = TALKING comes to no conclusion, but arbitrarily stops. Which is better, TO HIMSELF

LIZA EXPRESSES EMPATHY TOWARD THE UM HAVING OBSERVED THE SQUALOR IN WHICH HE LIVES. AND HIS BOUTS OF PETTY SQUABLING WITH APOLLON.

he asks, a cheap happiness or lofty suffering? Humiliation, such
as he has passed on to Liza, at least involves an acute
heightening of consciousness.

*   *   *

The Underground Man's restless chattering revels gleefully
in contradiction. He campaigns against determinism, and
champions capricious acts of malice – such as his payment to
Liza – as a form of rebellion against the tyranny of reason. Yet
he associates the 'sweetness' of 'free' wrongdoing with the
fantasy that 'you could not escape, you could not make yourself
into a different person' (1.2). And he is shown as trapped in the
same stale behaviour patterns. He is split between the desire for
solitude and the desire for company. He regards himself as
blessed, but also as cursed, by his unusual degree of self-
consciousness.

He is also divided between the self-effacement implied by
living in the 'underground' and the assertiveness and self-
advertisement he shows when he leaves it, and when he writes
his 'Notes'. He is half puritan, half romantic debauchee. He
describes a friendship in which he wanted unlimited power over
his friend's heart, and, when he got it, discarded the boy with
contempt (2.3). He behaves to Liza, too, as if she were either
pure love-object or filthy scum. He gravitates towards polarities –
'Either a hero or dirt, there was nothing in between' (2.2). He
is to be either far better than everyone else, or far worse. His
responsibility for his world is either made absolute – or
abolished.

We might say that the Underground Man is both a duellist
and a dualist. That is to say, he challenges the officer,
Ferfichkin, Zverkov and us, his readers, to single combat; he is
at war with everyone. And he is also a dualist, in that he
perceives his world in terms of striking extremes, polarities,
antinomies. Both his psychology and his philosophy are addicted
to the warfare between opposites.

Among many possible readings I shall single out two. Walter
Kaufmann has pointed out (1956, p. 12) that, though Dostoevsky
was in no sense an existentialist – the word did not come into
existence for another fifty years – *Notes from Underground* reads as
'the best overture to existentialism ever written'. For all the

existentialism borders on ~~the~~ an absurd and satyrical ~~new~~ concept of ~~the~~ truth thus promoting a irrational approach through reason to please oneself

Dialectic, logical argumentation is thereby refuted. ✱

shrill sickness of his hero, Dostoevsky shows us that 'individuality is wretched and revolting and yet, for all its misery, the highest good'. This is a dangerous half-truth – the more so in a period when Dostoevsky has been taken over by a pop-existentialism, the tenets of which, 'apparently so pitiless and so searching, have become', according to John Bayley, 'the opiate of the sub-intelligentsia, the props on which the common reader interested in ideas can cheerfully recline'.[7] The argument that *Notes* prefigures existentialism by championing a pre-rational freedom expressed in acts of caprice and perversity is only half the story. Nietzsche himself, after his initial enthusiasm, was to understand this (Frank, 1983, p. 149n). The existentialist commentators, from Shestov on, are right to see that Dostoevsky criticises a rational egoism. To seek to replace this by an *irrational egoism*, however, is scarcely a notable improvement. In place of a pseudo-scientific selfishness treating others as pawns, we are offered a purely private, irrational selfishness, which treats others as foes. In fact *Notes from Underground* represents a dialectic with a missing third term. The missing term is the Christian love-ethic ✱ namely through which Dostoevsky wished to show what might have helped his anti-hero. Its absence is due to censorship. 'Those swines of censors,' Dostoevsky complained to his brother Mikhail, 'where I mocked at everything and sometimes blasphemed for form's sake – that's let pass, but where from all this I deduced the need of faith and Christ – that is suppressed' (Mochulsky, 1971, p. 256). In a journal passage exactly contemporary with *Notes*, Dostoevsky wrote of the difficult, perhaps impossible, Christian ideal of loving one's neighbour as oneself and added, 'After Christ's appearance, it became clear that the highest development of personality must attain to that point where man *annihilates his own "I"*, surrenders it completely to all and everyone without reserve' (*Journal*, 16 April 1864). And in later life he spoke of the problem of the Underground Man as being that he lacked any sense of the holy. This is scarcely the unfettered creed of individuality at all costs hinted at by Kaufmann.

There are traces in the published story of what Dostoevsky intended. In chapter 1, section 11, the Underground Man opposes to the underground a vision of 'something different, entirely different, which I am eager for but shall never find', and imagines his readers charging him, with some justice, of

Christian love ethic ✱ – this would involve by relinquishing / becoming self-sacrificing
selfish attitude.
capricious
trained

having 'truth, but no virtue . . . without a pure heart there can be no full, correct understanding'. And in the terrible pages of his encounter with Liza he movingly bursts out with 'I'm incapable of being . . . good' (2.9).

The most interesting fact about the missing 'moral' of the tale, however, is that, just as in *Crime and Punishment*, Dostoevsky had later opportunities to reinstate his Christian theme, but desisted. Why? There is no easily available answer. To the contemporary reader, nevertheless, it is precisely the open-endedness of the tale that affords the reader with the perplexing and exciting sense of freedom that is both subversive and typically modern. In this way it could be said that the tale enacts the very dualism it defends, allowing us no absolute safety in any reading.

The Underground Man's complaint against most philosophical and political blueprints is that they ignore the rich and untamable contradictions of real life or 'living life'. The romantic in his idyll preserves his self like a 'jewel in cotton-wool'; the rationalist ignores man's unconscious; finally, a dependence on books causes Russians everywhere to neglect all that 'literature' fails to take into account. In his own life, in his 'hysterical thirst for contradictions and contrasts', the Underground Man is setting himself up as a brave explorer of that 'living life'.

And yet one way in which we can use the interpretative freedom the tale awards us is to see how deprived the Underground Man ultimately is of his own. So far from being the paragon of pre-rational free will extolled in pop-existentialism, he is man in hell, a man enslaved. In a real sense he is tormented by the idea of perfection, so often does he feel the need to attack it. He is also the victim of his own personality, which he can neither understand, control nor change. As he keeps boasting, his behaviour seems to be free of his reason. What this actually comes to mean is not 'freedom' but that he is motored by the same stale dreams and fantasies, by his mechanical pleasure in hurting and being hurt, by his inability either to accept or give love. He comically describes his earliest fantasies, thus: 'I triumphed over everybody; everybody else was routed and compelled to recognize my supremacy voluntarily, and I forgave them all. I, a famous poet and a courtier, fell in love; I received countless millions, and immediately bestowed them on the whole human race, at the same time confessing all my shameful deeds to the world . . .' (2.2). Freud said that he owed his discovery of the unconscious to the poets, and his admiration of Dostoevsky is well known.[8] Dostoevsky, in *Notes from Underground*, provides us with a modern map of the unconscious itself, in a devastating portrait anonymous enough to sit in for us all. Here is its Luciferian self-love and self-hatred, its exaggerated pride and vanity, its Eros comingling power and desire, its pointless, seemingly endless rage against the world and the self, its desire to protect itself against any possibility of change, and its furious need to revenge itself on the judgement that a 'higher' nature might pass on it. The frozen immobility of the underground is the stagnation and claustrophobia of the under-conscious self, which likes to meditate on revenge and nurse grievances with 'cold, venomous and above all undying resentment' (1.3), and feels a constant impulse to protect itself by retreating into life-myths of fantasy and unreason.

The crucial fact about the Underground Man here is that he has always been 'barbarously solitary' (2.1.). His solitude is as much a judgement on himself as on his society, a refusal of maturity or any affectionate obligation. He attacked those rationalists who left out of account any appeal to the empirical, to 'living life'. They preferred not to be discomforted by evidence that might untidy their selective abstracting processes. Yet he too is in retreat from uncertainty, indignity, shapelessness and confusion. He attacks fantasy, but embodies it. The underground is a place from which 'living life' can be identified but not inhabited. From it, the world appears structured entirely in terms of power, so that everyone is either monarch or bully, without true mutuality, and social relations seem a kind of persecution. If *Notes from Underground* is a good overture [OR PRELUDE] to 'existentialism', it is also a most cogent rebuke. [MOVES AWAY FROM EXISTENTIALYSM AND]

IS THERE ANY EVIDENCE up THAT THE UM CONVERTS TO CHRISTIANITY? MUST READ NOTES FROM UNDERGROUND TO FIND OUT.

3

Crime and Punishment (1866)

Notes from Underground, the prologue to the four great novels, is a dress rehearsal for *Crime and Punishment* in particular. Like the Underground Man, Raskolnikov is a soured or perverted idealist who has absorbed many modish new ideas and who is offered spiritual regeneration through a relationship with a prostitute. There are some hundred references to Raskolnikov's isolation. At the beginning he describes himself as 'lying about all day long in that beastly hole and thinking – thinking all sorts of absurd things' (i.1); at the end he describes his having sat 'skulking in my room like a spider' (v.4). This echoes the Underground Man, as does Raskolnikov's 'doubleness'. Richard Peace has excellently said that doubleness is both Dostoevsky's artistic method and also his polemical theme (1971, p. 33). In *Crime and Punishment* Dostoevsky explores the doubleness of Raskolnikov's character and passes on a sense of tortured ambivalence to the reader. We identify with this hero in a way that was impossible with the Underground man, an identification vexed by the fact that he is a murderer. We exult in Raskolnikov and abhor him, wish to see him punished and desire to see him escape. De Quincey praised Shakespeare for exploring, in *Macbeth*, the psychology of a murderer rather than a victim.[9] His praise marks a significant moment in Romantic aesthetics and one whose emotional logic *Crime and Punishment* pushes to its furthest point. Both Macbeth and Raskolnikov are victims of their own perverse psychology. In identifying so powerfully with Raskolnikov and simultaneously being so repelled by him, the reader has set up within him a tortured doubleness comparable to that by which Raskolnikov feels eaten alive. The suspense and excitement of reading *Crime and*

42

Punishment – a haunted and horrible excitement – are like that of no other novel.

Raskolnikov is a twenty-three-year-old former law-student, remarkably handsome, raggedly dressed and impoverished, from a *petit bourgeois* background. He lives in a tiny coffin-like cell of a room, whose claustrophobia seems a concrete metaphor for his state of mind. In this room he broods and plots the murder of an old pawnbroker. He dreams of murder as an expression of various new ideas he has promiscuously absorbed, which Dostoevsky termed 'half-baked' (Peace, 1971, p. 25); and as an idealistic act of justice. A number of coincidences conspire to give his plan energy and life. He receives a letter from his destitute mother, from which he learns that his beloved sister Dunya is to sacrifice herself in marriage to an uncaring businessman, Luzhin, to save the family fortunes. Raskolnikov's chosen victim, Alyona Ivanovna, appears, when he visits her at the start of the tale, morally debased, and he learns through a chance conversation that she will be alone at a particular hour. And he overhears a second idle conversation, between an officer and a student, who argue that she is a worthless creature who deserves no better and whose murder could be justified as the means to an end. This, terrifyingly, echoes the debate in his head and seems to give him external justification, showing that his ideas have general currency. He is throughout partly presented to us as a generous man maddened by the suffering and injustice he everywhere encounters.

In a breathtaking sequence in part I, he murders the old woman with a hatchet and takes some items left in pawn. Her innocent sister Lizaveta returns while he is searching the flat – he has forgotten to lock the door – and he murders her too, very horribly, and then, more by luck than good planning, escapes. He helps the family of an alcoholic, Marmeladov, who is run down by a carriage and killed, and engenders the devotion of his daughter Sonya, who has been driven into prostitution.

At the end of part II, Raskolnikov's mother and sister arrive in Petersburg. Dunya has been governess in the household of a curious degenerate called Svidrigaylov, who has fallen in love with her and tormented her with his attentions. She is now courted by the pompous businessman Luzhin, with whom Raskolnikov quarrels. His dislike of Luzhin triggers a scene in which Dunya is able to reject him. The entire Raskolnikov family – mother, daughter, son – are helped by Raskolnikov's innocent, good-hearted friend Razumikhin, who falls in love with Dunya. Raskolnikov's behaviour appears increasingly strange. He is carrying an extraordinary burden of obsession, mental pain and disturbance, which has cut him off in a private hell. The police suspect him but lack the evidence to prosecute, and there are three interviews between Raskolnikov and the investigator Porfiry, accompanied by much complex psychological warfare. Finally Raskolnikov finds himself shadowed equally by the morally ugly Svidrigaylov and the good Sonya, who mirror at this point the better and worse possibilities in his nature. Svidrigaylov wishes to enjoy the spectacle of his fellow transgressor's unusual sin, and to use this knowledge to blackmail Dunya into submission. Sonya wishes Raskolnikov to give himself up and reform through suffering. Meeting Dunya's resistance, Svidrigaylov shoots himself. Raskolnikov gives himself up and Sonya follows him to an eight-year term of imprisonment in Siberia.

Dostoevsky's genius is to show the interaction of ideas and personality. His characters do not incarnate philosophical positions: they demonstrate what it is like to be bitten by beliefs. *Raskol'nik* means heretic or schismatic, and there are a number of strands to Raskolnikov's heretical thinking. Like many a nineteenth-century intellectual from Carlyle to Nietzsche, he has a cult of Napoleon and a belief in the historical destiny of great and solitary heroes. In his first conversation with Porfiry, in part 3, Raskolnikov discusses an article he has written, claiming that the mass of men must lead lives of slavish obedience to the moral law. The unusual few, however, are entitled to 'step over' or transgress morality, in the name of a better future. The Russian word for 'crime' in the title – *prestuplenie* – also means 'stepping over' or transgression; and the book is full of transgressors.

In part III Razumikhin forcibly attacks the bad faith of Raskolnikov's belief in the all-importance of environment (ch. 5). Its insincerity springs from its being accompanied by a facile utopianism, which simultaneously proclaims that social conditions can be suddenly and irreversibly changed – stepped over. This facile marriage between determinism and idealism makes an explosive cocktail, and one that is still recognisable today. It marks, in a sense, our Romantic inheritance.

Raskolnikov believes that most men are wholly determined slaves, while the few are wholly free; the past has been wholly determined, but the future might be free. He is, in a strict sense, a Romantic moralist, given to making his responsibility for what surrounds him alternately absolute, and then abolishing it. He is also, throughout, a Romantic solitary. Although he worked hard as a student, no one apart from Razumikhin much liked him; by the end, in Siberia, he is equally unpopular with his fellow convicts.

In his confession to Sonya in part VI he outlines a number of different motives for his killing. He killed, he tells the appalled girl, because he had a wicked heart. He killed because he 'wanted to become a Napoleon' (ch. 4), and explains that he discovered he was no such thing. A Napoleon would have been less squeamish than he turned out to be, and he now judges himself one of those pretentious, mediocre people whose scruples render their ambitions powerless. Sonya gently punctures his intellectualising by inviting him to talk directly, 'without any examples'. He then explains how poor he and his family were, and how poverty endangered his sister. Throughout this conversation Sonya tries to get him to imagine his own act fully, without cheap theorising. But he insists he only killed 'a useless, nasty, harmful louse'. Thus, although he also characterises himself to her as 'vain, envious, spiteful, odious, vindictive', he still thinks his beliefs uncompromised. It is simply that he has been unmasked by his own act as unheroic, one of the mass, not a Napoleon after all. He rarely recalls that he also killed the gentle, simple Lizaveta, who, incidentally, once mended a shirt of his, and who was, significantly, the gentle Sonya's friend: they had exchanged crosses. Despite the pretence of wishing to become a benefactor of mankind by gaining wealth and power, he murdered – he tells Sonya – as an act of self-discovery, to find out whether he were 'vermin' or, on the other hand, had the 'right to kill'.

Razumikhin has argued that even a Napoleon would be punished by conscience (III.5): for him there is no world outside morality. And, indeed, Sonya at once intuits the damage Raskolnikov has inflicted on himself: 'What have you done to yourself?' He comes to see that he has killed himself, 'not the old hag'.

Much of the book's power comes from its exploration of

Raskolnikov's states of mind. His sense of isolation and 'bitter contempt' (i.1) for other people precede the murder. His punishment starts with his premeditation. Before the actual crime he already feels terror, suffers from nightmares and a sense of exclusion. He has cut himself off from his shy landlady, to whom he is in debt, and to whose strange, other-worldly daughter he was engaged before her death. In murdering his own better instincts he finds contact even with his own family, whom he loves, intolerable. 'Leave me alone, leave me alone, all of you. . . . I want to be alone, alone, alone', he cries to his visitors, in psychological torture (ii.5). The plea to be left alone becomes his *Leitmotiv*, repeated some dozen times. He has cut himself off from the human family, and, while he finds his solitude intolerable, contact with others is even worse.

Raskolnikov, apostle of the new creed of 'rational egoism', believes himself to be both free and wholly powered by reason. He is shown to be neither. He carries out the murder as if blindly propelled, and repeatedly feels that he 'no longer possessed any freedom of reasoning or will' (i.5) – the hand that holds the hatchet falling 'mechanically'. His behaviour in the pawnbroker's flat combines animal cunning with childish carelessness, so that, forgetting to lock the door, he feels forced to commit the second, horribly brutal, gratuitous murder, splitting open Lizaveta's head, full-face. She does not so much as protect herself. Even his robbery is incompetent: he steals a few items and a purse whose contents he never examines, hiding all of this roughly under a stone, but missing 1500 rubles in gold. He experiences the waking nightmare of visitors who knock on the door while he waits in animal terror on the other side.

Afterwards he is for a while delirious, subject to violent fits of emotion which exhaust him and render the outer world invisible. On the novel's second page the inner drama of his feelings is so powerful as to render the outer world invisible. By the last part (vi) his reverie is so deep that he horrifies his sister Dunya by passing her without recognising her (ch. 5). His self-absorption has here the consequence that Dunya is handed over to the lecherous Svidrigaylov, who attempts to rape her. And it was, paradoxically, exactly the danger to his sister from Svidrigaylov that he was lost in brooding about: his inner isolation has deprived him of any sense of the actual world. Throughout the tale he has the habit of walking suddenly away from his interlocutors, as if they had become suddenly invisible to him.

He is an aesthetic puritan and a political Romantic, and in both of these is characterised by an extreme impatience with the intractable, untidy facts of the world he inhabits. On his way to commit the murder he is redesigning the city, seeking to improve it both by fountains and by exterminating 'vermin'. The astute Porfiry three times typifies him as 'impatient', 'above all, impatient' (VI.2). This impatience has its generous side: he is capable of self-forgetting acts of compassion, and is throughout the tale, considering his own poverty, quixotically generous with most cases of need that he meets, from the Marmeladovs, to whom he gives twenty rubles, to passing beggars. He is maddened by the distress he everywhere encounters. Yet the same impatience is also connected to what the comfort-loving police doctor Zossimov calls his 'exceptional, insane vanity' (III.2), a description shortly afterwards endorsed by the dependable Razumikhin. He can respond to emotional distress in strangers and yet appear callous to those closest to him. Idealism itself comes to seem, in him, a kind of vanity.

What his impatient vanity ignores is his own fallen nature, his deep irrationality, and this is brought home to him in the way that his emotions now turn on him and victimise him. In an acute description Razumikhin notes his doubleness, as if there were two, diametrically opposed persons in him, each taking charge by turns – one of them moody, the other coldly, inhumanly callous (III.2).

He now becomes the puppet of his own feelings, the passive theatre for a procession of intense emotions – chiefly rage, disgust, joy – that he can neither predict nor understand. He experiences rage with Nastasya, when her presence upsets his plans for stealing the hatchet; and later with Razumikhin, into whose rooms he has blundered. His will is estranged from him. He intermittently loses the sense of his own body (I.6). He repeatedly experiences his own motives as dark to him, feeling mocked by his inability to decide whether he has visited Razumikhin out of free will or by chance. This lends the story its extraordinary mixed atmosphere of 'spur-of-the-moment impulse with trance-like inevitability' (J. Jones, 1983, p. 230).

I mentioned Raskolnikov's aesthetic puritanism. He is marked by puritanical disgust, with himself and with the world –

disgust at the wizened Alyona with her thin neck, like a chicken's leg, her colourless hair, her coughing and groaning. We might well say that he murders to kill his disgust, but finds he has thereby given it a terrible new vigour. He now feels disgust not merely at her corpse but also with her sister's murder, and then with himself for engendering both. Disgust now begins to colour all his relations, disgust that is 'malevolent, obstinate, virulent' (II.2). He finds he wishes to spit at or bite those he passes. 'He hated the people he met in the street, he hated their faces, the way they walked, the way they moved' (II.2). The adjectives 'squeamish', 'fastidious' are throughout associated with him, and even in his last interview with Dunya he is still defending the purely aesthetic point of view which would make the proper management of squeamishness, rather than the proper education of compassion, an adequate leading criterion in human affairs.

In committing his crime he has fatally damaged his own squeamishness, which is to say here his self-respect, his hypersensitive pride. The wound does not liberate him, but suppurates, making his self-alienation more deadly. A. D. Nuttall has pointed out (1978, p. 49) that Raskolnikov's unconscious does not simply act as a Freudian repository of dark, selfish desire, but 'his dark side is his light side and his light side dark. In [his] dreams pity and love surge up with more than libidinal ferocity', as, for example, in his piteous dream of the mare beaten to death. His unconscious repeatedly tries to betray him into exposing his own guilt; and, since his only spiritual hope lies in confession and punishment, is in this on the side of his future redemption. (Because we sense that the pain of claiming full responsibility for his crime will be terrible, we both dread his confession, suffering an intense claustrophobia awaiting it, and experience a welcome discharge of tension when it comes.) So, hearing a discussion of the murder at the police station, Raskolnikov faints, as if his unconscious wished to unmask and revenge itself on his 'rational', conscious self. Again, meeting the police clerk Zamyotov in a bar, he experiences the urge to stick his tongue out at him, metaphorically speaking, and sails close to the wind. 'What if it was I who murdered the old woman and Lizaveta?' he taunts the man (II.6). He repeats the perverse pleasure of endangering himself when overwhelmed by 'an inexplicable and irresistible impulse' to revisit the old woman's flat (II.6), procuring a dangerous thrill out of provoking the workmen there as outrageously as he is able, asking them why the blood has been removed, daring them to take him to the police station. Again with Porfiry he is caught between a 'rational' desire for freedom and the deep 'irrational' desire for punishment and atonement, a split with which Porfiry brilliantly plays.

In his self-estrangement, he also alternates between fits of sudden joy and devastating bouts of apathetic depression. He feels joy when he realises that he has retained the cunning necessary to examine his clothing for tell-tale blood stains, 'animal joy' when, at the police station the following day, he finds that he has been summoned merely for non-payment of debts, not murder; joy after hiding the valuables, and inexpressible joy when, after he has generously helped at Marmeladov's death-scene, the child Polya reaches out and touches his heart with gratitude. Yet, after he has excitedly tried to save a drunken young girl from the aged rake who hounds her, he gives in to equally sudden despair – 'Let them devour each other alive for all I care' – reflecting that it is essential that a 'percentage' of girls must go to the devil (I.4). The same shift of mood accompanies his excited advice to Dunya (III.2) not to marry Luzhin, once more followed by 'Marry whom you like for all I care' as he relapses into a near-autistic state of desolation.

Raskolnikov starts the book in the guise of Byronic *poseur*, 'morose, gloomy, proud, stuck-up' (III.2), vain about the distance separating him from ordinary mortals, though not incapable of empathy for them. After the murder his separation bites in earnest and he becomes a man in hell. He feels that the world is 'dead and indifferent to him *alone*' (II.6; emphasis added). With the triumph of his worse self he alienates all but the Christ-like Sonya. Even his mother feels panic-stricken about meeting him (III.3) and crosses herself in terror at his approach. He has started to resemble the bogyman Svidrigaylov, at whose arrival small children scatter in terror.

*   *   *

Raskolnikov's story is given to us in a number of different contexts. There is the city of St Petersburg itself, and then the other characters, who, while acting as foils and augmenting aspects of Raskolnikov's predicament, are also vivid and fascinating in their own right. Dostoevsky wrote that he had his 'own view of art, and that which the majority call fantastic and exceptional is for me the very essence of reality' (*Letters*, 10 March 1869). His fantastic realism colours his depiction of place, as well as his use of dream and coincidence. This is not at all the spacious baroque Petersburg of neoclassical prints, all mighty prospects and stately grandeur. Instead it is a city of the mind, nightmarish, full of drunks and beggars, stifling and stinking in the summer heat, full of diverse yet uniquely horrible smells, racked with pain and squalor. Raskolnikov's mother complains that the city as a whole is as oppressive as – in a sense is an extension of – her son's tiny and terrible room. 'Oh, but where's one to get a breath of fresh air here? It's as bad in the streets as in a room with closed windows. Heavens, what a town!' (III.3).

In this nightmare town, everything is a nightmare yellow, 'a colour with a stronger connotation of dirt in Russian than in English' (J. Jones, 1983, p. 205). Yellow is the colour of faces – Porfiry's, Raskolnikov's, both Mr and Mrs Marmeladov's in their last moments, and an anonymous suicide's; of rooms – Svidrigaylov's, Alyona's, Raskolnikov's, and of the wooden houses Svidrigaylov passes on the way to his death; and objects – a banknote, a prostitute's certificate, the sugar Nastasya brings Raskolnikov for his tea, Marmeladov's wound when he is run over, and of the 'yellow water in a yellow glass' offered Raskolnikov when he faints in the police station.

It is, moreover, a city of bullies and victims, with only rare glimpses of light and compassion. The Underground Man presented social relations as a form of persecution, but inhabited a social vacuum. Here the social world is realised in some detail and there are a host of small, intimate, painful cameos of cruelty. Serfdom had been abolished in 1861; but cruelty, perversity and exploitation survive. 'Crushed' and 'humiliated' – those essential Dostoevskian adjectives – have much work to do. Women are often the helpless victims. The pawnbroker Alyona has bullied and beaten her meek sister Lizaveta, who, though unmarried, is often pregnant, into total subjection, on one occasion nearly biting off Lizaveta's finger in her rage. Sonya is sacrificed to prostitution to save her family from starving; and Raskolnikov's sister Dunya is also at risk, both from Svidrigaylov's attentions and from the odious Luzhin, to whom, to save herself, she is to be sold in a loveless marriage. Raskolnikov even fears that Dunya might sink to Sonya's level, as might Sonya's half-sister Polya. 'Children can't stay children in St Petersburg', he bitterly complains to Sonya (iv.4). In part I he watches a fat elderly dandy hovering predatorily about a fifteen-year-old girl who has been made drunk and raped. He intervenes energetically, calling out, by an association of ideas, 'Hey you! Svidrigaylov!' (for the latter has a developed taste in young girls), before giving in to cynical despair. The little scene is echoed in part II when he watches a down-trodden fifteen-year-old singer, once more surveyed by an elderly (perhaps innocent) gentleman. Shortly after this he passes a large group of middle-aged women, most of whom have a black eye.

It is a world of destitution, despair and suicide. Dunya arrives in the city with her gloves in holes, her and her mother's clothes much patched and mended, and they have only three rubles left between them. The Kapernaumov family, landlords to Sonya, all live in one room. Here, as in the far wealthier and grander world of *The Idiot*, Dostoevsky shows no special sympathy for the rich. The wealthy Luzhin is repulsive, and even the devilish Svidrigaylov seems to gain in Dostoevsky's esteem for having once been carelessly imprisoned for debt. In part II Raskolnikov sees a woman rescued from drowning who had lately attempted to hang herself. Both Raskolnikov and Sonya contemplate suicide. Svidrigaylov not merely commits suicide himself, but is associated throughout with murder, or with complicity in the suicide of others, and feels haunted by his victims. He is the book's leading agent of humiliation, and its leading philosopher too.

This is the *shapeliest* novel Dostoevsky was to write. Here he uses a detailed elaboration of small scenes that suggests a longer time-span than is in fact presented. The events of the entire novel occupy – startlingly – little more than a week. It is as though the book moved in two, apparently opposite but related, temporal modes: an 'existential' present, weightless yet intense, thrilling, terrifying, embarrassing and comically grotesque by turns; and the vision of eternity, seen by Raskolnikov as a square metre of rock on which a man might for ever be trapped and yet be grateful to survive, and, later, by

Svidrigaylov, as a provincial bath-house, dusty and full of spiders. These longer perspectives open out on the present without increasing its stock of light or air. They merely heighten the mood of inane horror and oppression. The book presents something like a vision of hell.

Dream and coincidence accompany temporal compression. 'Many characters are found living alongside one another in the most improbable way. Thus Svidrigaylov lodges next door to Sonya; Luzhin lives with Lebezyatnikov who in turn lives in the same house as the Marmeladov family . . . Luzhin is related to Svidrigaylov . . . and is the former guardian of Lebezyatnikov; Porfiry is related to Razumikhin' (Peace, 1971, p. 38). This helps give the novel its formal intensity and emotional claustrophobia. Thus, when Raskolnikov in part VI decides to seek out Svidrigaylov, he at once stumbles on him, as if he were seeking an aspect of his own mind – which is, in fact, precisely what he is to discover.

And the book is full of dreams. Raskolnikov early refers to his plan of murdering the old pawnbroker as 'this damnable dream of mine' (I.5). And his plan of murder is only disclosed to the reader after his terrifying nightmare of a mare being savagely beaten to death by peasants. In this dream Raskolnikov is both the dream-child impotent to halt the violence he watches with tormented pity, the peasant – since he will shortly commit an act of violence himself – and, lastly, the mare itself, in that he also sees himself as the degraded and brutalised victim of circumstance. Later he dreams of attempting to murder the old woman again, while she soundlessly laughs and the room grows full of a whispering, laughing and finally silent, waiting crowd (III.6). One consequence of his crime is that he now finds it increasingly hard to tell dream-states from waking ones, so that, when Svidrigaylov first appears, he is unsure whether he is not dreaming him. Svidrigaylov has his own nightmares, too.

The good Razumikhin is Raskolnikov's most obvious foil and the reader's touchstone. His name comes from *razhum*, 'reason'. Like Horatio and Hamlet the two have both been students, and Razumikhin plays the role of benignly intelligent onlooker to Raskolnikov's mental fevers, pondering whether he is mad or a political conspirator (VI.1). His simple heart is set against Raskolnikov's devious one, and his easy love of and belief in good things opposes his friend's pretentious asceticism. He is

twice heard comically, but after all sensibly, declaiming about
pies – 'a luscious pie' – with all the gusto of a character in
Dickens. Above all, by sticking to the student life, with all its
poverty and humiliation, he shows how *willed* Raskolnikov's
'dropping-out' has been. 'I could have got lessons for half a
ruble an hour. After all, there's Razumikhin. He manages to
get work' (v.4). Razumikhin has fallen deeply in love with
Dunya, but lacks the confidence to press his suit. One of
Raskolnikov's decent acts is to bring the two closer, bequeathing
them, in effect, each to the other. Warm-hearted, frank, jolly,
open and guileless, honest and strong as a giant – Dostoevsky's
idealised picture of a good Russian soul – Razumikhin is baffled
by Raskolnikov's caprices, and criticises his plagiaristic, over-
literary *persona* (II.6). He pleads for a tolerance of man's
imperfections – 'By talking rot you get at the truth' (III.1).

In an elegant, subtle argument Richard Peace suggests that
the other characters symbolise aspects of Raskolnikov's dualism.
Raskolnikov has both a ruthless and a meek side, and expresses
each by turn. Early events mirror this oscillation. After he visits
the 'ruthless, self-interested Alyona, he next meets the squirming,
self-effacing Marmeladov; in a letter from home he reads that
the self-sacrificing Dunya has escaped the clutches of the
ruthless Svidrigaylov only to fall into the hands of the equally
ruthless Luzhin . . .' (Peace, 1971, p. 35). Raskolnikov has
murdered his own better, i.e. meeker, self, as symbolised in his
wicked destruction of the harmless Lizaveta.

This is true, but does not account for the novel's 'superfluous'
energy and power, which have something to do with Dostoevsky's
own gleeful revelling in the dark side of his own case, and his
exultation in the untidy and indeterminate *for its own sake*, as
well as for 'moral' or rhetorical purposes. In this process
humour plays an important, neglected role.

The comic Marmeladov, in the second chapter, is the first of
a procession of total strangers who claim some kinship with
Raskolnikov, and with whom he at once falls into intimacy. He
is a fifty-year-old balding drunkard with tiny eyes and a bloated
face. One literary source appears to be Micawber in Dickens's
David Copperfield. He has fat red hands with black nails, and is
covered with bits of hay. Having stolen his wife's savings, he
has been on a drunken spree, pawning his clothes and sleeping
rough for five days. He buttonholes Raskolnikov, starting a

bizarre, soul-baring confession that is part lamentation, part family history, part boastful self-abasement. He drinks in order to suffer, he announces. And his love of suffering extends to his pleasure in being beaten by his wife and pulled by the hair. This is a second marriage for both him and his wife, and she married him only because she had 'nowhere to go'. Sonya, his child by his first marriage, is beaten by Mrs Marmeladov, just as her first husband beat her. Marmeladov provokes titters by announcing that Sonya has been forced onto the streets, and his extravagant confession, which is funny and horrible in equal parts, sets the tone of the book, from which humour, however black, is rarely absent for long.

The humour often seizes on some contingent detail that Dostoevsky startles us into imagining, whose naked inadvertency strikes us as (in some combination) ludicrous, painful, funny, horrible: for example, Marmeladov crawling 'meekly' on his knees to make it easier for his wife to drag him by the hair, and shouting out that he enjoys it; or the absurd and touching pride Mrs Marmeladov feels in a 'certificate of good conduct' which enshrines what is left of her self-respect and which surfaces repeatedly, at the riotously farcical funeral meal she stages when Marmeladov is dead, and, mysteriously, at her own death-bed. Or Mrs Marmeladov jeering at Sonya's virginity; 'What are you keeping it for? What a treasure!'

D. H. Lawrence derisively called Dostoevsky's characters 'fallen angels' (cited in Lord, 1970, p. 8). But there is something extraordinary in how Dostoevsky retains our sympathy for the potential nobility of characters whom he simultaneously shows us grotesquely undoing their own dignity. Marmeladov's weakness is real, and his family are made wretched because of it, and yet Dostoevsky partly values him because his drunkard's love of self-exposure and self-laceration forces the reader to take a closer than ordinary look at pain. His shameless parading of his humility is half insincere and grotesque and yet – compare, for example, the more irredeemably bogus Luzhin – has something authentic about it. 'Behold the man!' he blasphemously proclaims of himself, echoing Pilate's presentation of the bound and suffering Christ in John 19:5, before daring Raskolnikov to tell him he is not 'a dirty swine'. He foreshadows Raskolnikov's own acceptance of suffering at the end, and shows how ambiguous an act such acceptance can be.

The quality of Christian humility is always, in Dostoevsky, opposed to solipsism and a proud, separate self-exposure. It is startling to learn (III.3) that Raskolnikov's cell has a window. It is mentioned only once, and no one looks out of it. The shock comes because his room seems to embody Raskolnikov's state of mind, which is oppressively without prospect of escape. Yet his is not the only windowless world. Marmeladov, although we meet him only briefly, puts a stagy Dickensian energy into a tiny repertoire of psychological routines. His wife Katerina, too, increasingly escapes reality through a retreat into fantasy, especially as her tuberculosis takes over. A generous-hearted woman, she has been maddened by poverty, illness, and her husband's drunken fecklessness. Even when her fantasies take a ludicrous more-than-Mrs-Nickleby-ish turn, Dostoevsky clearly delights in her capacity instantly to believe her own inventions. At her husband's death-bed she introduces Raskolnikov as a rich, well-connected young man known to her husband since he was a child. In fact the two have just met. By the riotous scene of the funeral meal for her husband he has turned into a man offered a university chair which everyone knew he was to take up in two years. Her exaggerated pride is funny, and her baffled idealism is moving. As with her husband, she raises the leading question of how to find an adequate moral style with which to suffer indignity. She parodies Raskolnikov's idealistic impatience when she is 'so *ferociously* anxious for everyone to live in peace and contentment and not *dare* to live otherwise, that the slightest jarring note and the smallest failure reduced her to frenzy' (v.2). She then quarrels frantically with her German landlady, who evicts her. Taking to the streets, she makes her terrified weeping children sing and dance to the sound of a frying-pan that she beats. She asks them to sing 'nice drawing-room songs', 'French songs', so onlookers will realise that they are children of 'good family' and find the spectacle more touching. Then, haemorrhaging from the throat, raving and singing, she dies in Sonya's room. 'They've driven the mare to death. I'm done for!' she shouts, with hatred and despair, and an echo of Raskolnikov's dream, as she dies.

In Katerina the creation of an autonomous world protects her few last rags of self-respect. Hers is a kind of heroic foolishness, and her death-bed scene, like that of her husband, at whom she screams peremptorily in her rage as he dies, is a triumph of depicted muddle – grotesque farce, pathos and horror all co-existing in a fine indeterminacy. Her fevered imaginings echo Raskolnikov's.

Poverty is not the only stimulus, however, to the creation of a windowless, private world. Some of Raskolnikov's views are parodied by the sententious, self-made Luzhin, arguably the most unpleasant character in Dostoevsky. Both champion 'rational egoism' and speak of humankind in the abstract, dehumanised language of 'percentages', and each outlaws pity, either in practice or in theory. It is as if Dostoevsky were suggesting an echo between capitalism and nihilism: neither offers any barrier against a wholly self-seeking and demonic individualism. Luzhin, the successful bourgeois, is the book's most self-deluded character. A pompous, wordy, self-absorbed fool, stylishly dressed with a dandy-like neatness – like a 'German on his wedding-day' (Dostoevsky disliked Germans) – with a lorgnette and massive gold ring, he spends hours when alone admiring himself in a looking-glass. He is a successful, self-made lawyer, and it can be no accident that Raskolnikov, too, studied law. Luzhin represents the hypocritical, officious bourgeois world against which Raskolnikov has rebelled, with its vindictive spite and meanness, and its fatuously touchy idiotic vanity. He wants to marry Dunya, over whom he lords it in his fantasies, because so beautiful a girl will help his social ascent, and because her extreme poverty will put her for ever in his debt. Dunya and her mother have travelled sixty miles in an open peasant's cart to take the train, and then, on arrival, have been put by Luzhin into disreputably poor lodgings. Raskolnikov at once instinctively hates Luzhin's meanness; and this, together with the 3000 rubles Dunya inherits from Svidrigaylov's wife, enables them to send him packing, in one of the book's few scenes in which indignity and persecution receive a just come-uppance.

The second such scene also concerns Luzhin, who has been guardian to the 'nihilist' Lebezyatnikov, by whom he fears he will be unmasked as a reactionary. His hatred of Raskolnikov is now such that, in order to hurt him through Sonya, he plants a 100-ruble note on the unwitting girl and then publicly accuses her of theft at Marmeladov's funeral meal. In the event he is unmasked, not for posing as one of the young generation, 'without prejudice', as he throughout fears, but as a dishonest, mean-minded villain, by both Lebezyatnikov, who observed the fraud, and Raskolnikov, who intuits its motivation.

It is a paradox that Dostoevsky, the most ideological of novelists, can so often convince us that he is exhibiting life rather than – unlike other novelists with a 'message' (for example, D. H. Lawrence) – bullying it into yielding up a moral. Here he sails close to the wind in showing both how general and how half-baked is the blight of new ideas by which Raskolnikov is infected. The phrase 'enlightened ideas', like the words 'rational' and 'high-minded', rarely occurs without irony. Here, even Sonya has been reading G. H. Lewes's *Physiology*, while Svidrigaylov, who plays major demon to Luzhin's minor one, while boasting that he is a lover of Schiller, fatuously announces that 'I put all my hopes in anatomy now' (IV.1), and identifies progress with the *can-can*. The book's spokesperson for radical pieties, however, is the clown Lebezyatnikov (*lebezit*, to fawn), a seedy, scrofulous man with whitish hair and mutton-chop whiskers. Like Luzhin he believes science has 'outlawed' pity and is against private charity. He parrots a hand-me-down mixture of utilitarianism, positivism and idealism, often directly echoing the radicals' handbook, Chernyshevsky's *What is to be Done?* There is still today a satisfyingly contemporary ring, however, about his manner of airily announcing that he has 'seen through' social protocol – for example, the custom of funeral meals; or that the society of the future will contain no violence, and will legislate free entry into rooms. (What if someone is on the lavatory? Luzhin wants to know.) His loony pronouncements range from the mysterious 'some people completely deny the existence of children', to his solemn communication that the French now cure lunatics by talking to them. His attitude to women is, to say the least, questionable. Nominally he is for emancipation, commending the communard Mrs Varentz who idiotically told her husband that she had to leave him since she could not forgive him for 'having deceived me by concealing from me the fact that there exists another form of society based on the commune'. He claims that he would *oblige* his wife to take a lover, to show his radical good faith. In fact, however, he has courted Sonya, and then abused and defamed her after being rejected, and announces that in the socialist paradise there will be rational prostitution since 'this is a woman's normal condition' (v.1). This looks forward

to the demonising of progressives in *The Devils*, but Lebezyatnikov
is a harmless fool by comparison.

The fight over Raskolnikov's fate is one with many corners to
it. Ultimately he has to choose for himself. What is distinctively
modern about the book, and about Dostoevsky, is that education
comes out of chaos, from the immersion in indeterminacy.
Raskolnikov is early presented to us as 'fond of abstract
reasoning and therefore cruel' (IV.4). The movement of the
book is to break down his faith in 'abstract reasoning', which is
related to his rational egoism, and to replace, in the words of
the epilogue, 'dialectics' with 'life'. He is shown repeatedly
offended by the indeterminacy and irrational confusion of the
world. He fulminates against the mixture of love and hate in his
sister, who of course exactly resembles him in this, and is
similarly amazed that shame and disgrace can co-exist so
comfortably with an intense moral beauty in Sonya (III.3). The
reader, too, finds it hard to believe that Sonya's degrading
occupation would long leave her so pure-of-heart. But the moral
point that the world (and he as part of it) is necessarily a more
contradictory – or dualistic – place than his 'rational' impatience
and disgust will allow him to see is made throughout, through
uncertainty, humour and paradox.

Porfiry, for example, uses uncertainty to bring Raskolnikov
to justice. The book is full of sleuths and sleuthing. Many of the
characters try to penetrate Raskolnikov's states of mind, and
Razumikhin, Sonya and Svidrigaylov are all, in this, amateur
detectives. But Porfiry is the soul-doctor among the book's
many sleuths. He is a tender-hearted detective of human souls,
snub-nosed like Socrates, and with a line in seemingly polite,
waggish chatter that flirts with intimacy without embracing it.
In (especially) the second of their three interviews, Raskolnikov
seeks definition in terms of power. He both wants to become
Porfiry's victim and dreads the idea. He is nearly caught
through Porfiry's self-withholding. He reads Porfiry's behaviour
as a sequence of ploys and gambits improvised to unnerve him
into a self-exposure he secretly desires. Porfiry intimately
understands his self-division, and their talk is full of feint and
double-bluff. Like Sonya, he advises Raskolnikov to help himself
by freely embracing suffering and thus rejoining the human
family.

Before he is ready to do so, however, he has a further struggle to undergo. At the start of part VI, when he knows Porfiry identifies him as the murderer but lacks the evidence to convict him, he finds himself seeking Svidrigaylov, who has also hinted strongly that he knows Raskolnikov's secret. Superficially, he seeks Svidrigaylov to discover what power the man has and what he intends with it. At a deeper level, he needs the meeting in order to understand *himself* more clearly. Until then he has a sense of moral weightlessness.

With his scarlet lips, piercingly blue eyes and love of adolescent girls, Svidrigaylov could have been a villain out of melodrama. Dostoevsky makes him more interesting. During his nightmare appearance at Raskolnikov's bedside in part IV, he ingratiatingly insists on his kinship with Raskolnikov – 'We are birds of a feather', he three times says. Raskolnikov experiences his sense of connection as a menace he cannot understand. Later in part IV we see him licking his lips over Sonya and Raskolnikov's first interview, on which he has eavesdropped. An epicure of depravity, who has run out of new sensations and thus suffers from terminal boredom, Svidrigaylov realises he has stumbled onto something that will stimulate his jaded palate, and that he can also use to blackmail Dunya with. Given that he has formerly used his sexual appetite exclusively for purposes of indulgence, his now genuinely passionate love of Dunya seems an apt punishment.

Svidrigaylov may have murdered his wife, and his servant Philip hanged himself. He feels haunted by both, and has played an uncertain role in each death, but is chillingly vague about the details. One fifteen-year-old girl he interfered with also hanged herself. By the end of the book he has procured for himself another fifteen-year-old as his fiancée, despite his wife's very recent demise. One secret of his power in the book comes from the fact that, in this dog-eat-dog world, he has a consistent explanation about why people behave as they do. All women, he tells Raskolnikov during their last colloquy, secretly love humiliation. His wife enjoyed his using his riding-whip on her. Even Dunya, he suggests, may have enjoyed his persecution of her more than she has publicly admitted. In every relationship, he tells Raskolnikov, there are areas so secret that they can never be disclosed.

His power thus stems from the fact that, as he puts it, *vice* is 'founded on nature and not subject to the whims of fancy . . .

always there in your blood, like a piece of red-hot coal' (vi.4). Indeed 'reason', he says (echoing David Hume), must be the slave of the passions. Not that his ethical pessimism is the last word: but he is there to show how large an area of the soul the rationalists leave unmapped. Unlike Raskolnikov, Svidrigaylov commits his crimes without (apparent) remorse. He seems to show what the class of Napoleonic supermen that Raskolnikov longs to join might actually, drearily, resemble. Raskolnikov has throughout preached the need for a 'new idea' and for the 'new men' who might enact it. Svidrigaylov shows us the search for the new as itself an old, old story, in the guise of a purely aesthetic or purely erotic search for sensation and novelty. He is a gourmet of novelty, and, echoing Raskolnikov himself, is associated with 'comfort and aesthetics' (vi.6) up to the moment of his death.

After Dunya's attempt to shoot him, in a scene of high melodrama, comes the intimate squalor of his last hours. He conducts a tour of duty, giving 3000 rubles to Sonya to save her from her life of prostitution, and 1500 to his fiancée. This springs from no special great-heartedness, as his kindness to two quarrelling clerks (vi.6) shows. He befriends them because each has a crooked nose, one bent to the left, one to the right: 'comfort and aesthetics' are what he lives and dies by, and he is trying out philanthropy in the same whimsical spirit with which he has tried out depravity. One of the last scenes he witnesses, through a hole in the wall of his hotel room, is a *vignette* of banal and squalid bullying between two men, as if the world-view he has spoken for and lived by were to imprison him to the end. He dreams of a mouse, of the dead girl he abused, and, finally and most memorably, of a five-year-old girl seductively made up, behaving grotesquely like a whore. He shoots himself in a watch-tower manned by a small Jewish soldier wearing an Achilles helmet, the note of mock-heroic sustained to the last.

Sonya, the book's chief representative of the Good, is an equally melodramatic conception. The good-hearted prostitute is a hackneyed figure who perhaps ought not to succeed as a character, and yet she is real to us. She has been criticised for being 'meek to the point of anaemia' and suffering from a sickly timidity (Hingley, 1962, p. 102). Dostoevsky's point would seem to be that, in a world of violent self-assertion, only an equally energetic self-abnegation can make amends. And she may be timid, but is certainly not at all weak. On her first appearance she is gaily tricked out with the uniform of her trade – second-hand gaudy silk dress, bright shoes and parasol, red-feathered hat – a tiny self-sacrificing figure with an unsullied heart. What prostitute in any English novel of the period is as vividly 'seen' as this? Unlike the book's many solipsists, she is awake to the needs of others, her face alive, in a marvellous phrase, with 'insatiable compassion' (IV.4). She at once intuits Raskolnikov's suffering and her horror is never at him, only at what he has done to himself. Her love partly (only) dissolves his hatred. 'What does God do for you?' he asks, and she unforgettably answers, 'He does everything.' It is impossible, she observes, for people to be just. And the fact that her love for him arouses, almost to the end, his anger and resentment, as well as his trust, is finely observed.

In Dostoevsky's mature tragi-comic vision, the most painful moments of the novel – for example the Marmeladov deaths – are sometimes also the funniest. Through humour Dostoevsky exhibits the sheer irrational confusion of life, but does so with a sense of tolerance, as well as of savage glee. His characters frequently combine extreme fastidiousness with a violent urge towards self-exposure. The humour comes, again and again, from the clash between these, so that we are exposed to a theatrical soul-baring at once shameless and shameful, our sense of separate self offended by immersion in the absurd particularity of lives other than our own. One example here comes to mind: the account (I.3) of Mrs Svidrigaylov copying out Dunya's 'noble' letter accusing her husband of neglecting his wife, and then going on to give public readings of this letter, for which queues are seen to form. Embarrassment, excitement and comedy all here accompany the ludicrous (multiple) act of self-disclosure. Moreover, the comedy highlights the prevailing opposition on which all the novels are built: between egoism and love. We laugh at the affront to our own *pudeur*, at the horrible clowning that draws us as readers steadily into acknowledging membership in a community of fools, and surrender a little of our own self-importance in so doing.

In Raskolnikov's case the opposition between a defensive 'separateness' and renunciation into community-in-sin is one on which his fate depends. He is, of course, self-divided to the end, refusing ever fully to acknowledge the wrong-headedness of his ideas. It may be to the good that Dostoevsky never completed the sequel that he planned about Raskolnikov's regeneration: intellectuals make unconvincing saints. And yet no one is wholly irredeemable either, and the incompleteness of the ending we possess is convincing too. His progress is marked by prostrations, as if he were starting a little to renounce his stubborn self-conceit. He prostrates himself before Sonya (IV.4), acknowledging her goodness, and later before his mother (VI.7); and, just before his final confession, falls to the ground as Sonya had counselled, to the hilarity of one onlooker but not of the reader. Raskolnikov's approximate self-surrender is carried out in character, into the epilogue in Siberia, where he has a prophetic nightmare of the bacillus of 'absolute' individuality that is to plague our own century.

4

The Idiot (1868)

The Idiot caused Dostoevsky more trouble than his other major novels. He wrote some seven drafts, which differ wildly in their plottings, and feared, after finishing, that he had expressed only a fraction of what he intended. The notoriously hard task he set himself was to depict a good man, and the question of success, in Dostoevsky's mind, was linked to the question of the comic. Both Don Quixote and Dickens's Mr Pickwick haunted the composition, and he noted that these figures are good only because they are ridiculous at the same time. Despite his fears, he did produce that 'pity aroused for the Good which is mocked and does not know its own value' (*Letters*, January 1868). Like all his great books, *The Idiot* is a flawed masterpiece, the best scenes of which have an unforgettable immediacy unavailable to more 'perfect' stylists. And the reader's sympathy, as in any good novel, is divided and mobilised on behalf of a number of characters.

The novel is in four parts with an epilogue. the first is the most shapely and striking, the hectically condensed action occurring in under twenty-four hours. Dostoevsky's genius flowered best in a compressed time-scheme. Prince Myshkin, the 'idiot' of the title, and a twenty-eight-year-old survivor of an ancient house, has spent four years, after a cruel upbringing, being treated for epilepsy by a Dr Schneider in a Swiss sanatorium. As the story opens he is found in a third-class railway carriage returning to St Petersburg, conversing with two representatives of the Russia he has lost touch with – Rogozhin, black-haired, white-faced, short, stocky, ill-educated, who has inherited a fortune from his rich merchant father; and Lebedev, red-nosed, pimply, a case-hardened, cynical low-grade civil servant, a grovelling lackey and court jester who hangs on Rogozhin's every word, since he realises the latter is rich, though Rogozhin ignores him. Myshkin is strangely dressed, cloaked and gaitered, blond and bearded, travelling almost without luggage. His physical description resembles that of Christ.

The plot will concern Myshkin's relations with two beautiful women, Nastasya Filipovna and Aglaya Yepanchin. The former is – or acts out the part of – a 'fallen woman'. The latter rebels against the role of pure young daughter of the bourgeoisie. As the novel opens, the Prince has heard of neither of these women. By the end of twenty-four hours he has attracted, and been attracted by, both, and has, moreover, been momentarily engaged to Nastasya and then jilted by her in favour of Rogozhin. Just as the Prince is divided throughout the tale between the two girls, so Nastasya oscillates between the Prince and the ferociously jealous, tormented Rogozhin.

Rogozhin is agitated on the train. He recounts how he stole money from his father to buy the beautiful Nastasya some earrings, and, when his father discovered this, he beat him and begged the jewels back off the girl. The Prince calms him down. The Prince next arrives at the home of his distant cousin Mrs Yepanchin. He accosts a suspicious footman, while he waits for General Yepanchin, and describes a guillotining to him. The footman likes Myshkin and yet is intensely indignant with him. This is to be a common reaction. Later we hear of a conversation between Myshkin and a waiter (II.5) about a murder. Myshkin, we gather, apprehends only other human beings around him, lacking the false seriousness of caste; while others perceive exclusively in terms of rank and wealth. (This is, incidentally, a simplicity that causes him later to misread 'Society' as glittering where it is actually full of hatred and vanity.) He disarms General Yepanchin's suspicions, partly by absorbing his rudeness without reacting to it, and shows him his calligraphic skills. The General hires him for his skills and recommends that he be lodged with the Ivolgins. Before proceeding to the Ivolgins' flat, he has an interview with Mrs Yepanchin and her three daughters, with whom he is equally successful and equally odd, recounting a mock execution and the tale of Marie, a woman seduced, abandoned and ostracised in the Swiss village where he lived, whom he befriended before her death, and whom he comforted by mobilising the support of the local children.

The energy of the book is now carried by the first two (of many) scenes of scandal, both instigated by Nastasya Filipovna. An orphan since the age of six, she has been cynically seduced, used and abandoned by her guardian, the cowardly egoist Totsky, who used to come down to stay with her for two months to 'dishonour, insult, excite and deprave her' (1.16). Drafts show that Dostoevsky originally intended Nastasya's seduction to be carried out by a male relative, and incest is a buried theme here. Totsky has betrayed his trust as a person *in loco parentis*, and exonerates himself with a farcical glibness on the grounds that, as an 'inveterate sensualist', he was clearly 'not responsible for his actions' (1.4). In the game of 'Truth' they play at her birthday party, Totsky boasts that his worst action ever was a sentimental masquerade involving camellias, rather than this act of cynical debauchery. Nastasya, as a result, takes upon herself the entire load of guilt and shame, made worse at the time the tale opens, since Totsky wishes to free himself from any claim she might have on him so that he can marry the eldest Yepanchin daughter. He therefore offers 75,000 rubles as her dowry, to bribe the unprincipled opportunist Ganya Ivolgin to marry her and thus take her off his hands. Nastasya knows that she is being 'sold' and that Ganya is interested solely in her money. Ganya affects Aglaya's hand, too, but she does not care for him either.

The first scandal occurs when Nastasya bursts, uninvited, into the Ivolgin household, ready to humiliate Ganya and his family in revenge for Ganya's readiness to buy her in a loveless marriage. She bursts in, pushing Myshkin aside as if he were a backward servant, impersonating a 'shameless hussy' to antagonise the impoverished Ivolgins, who are forced, as she knows, to take in lodgers as a result of General Ivolgin's drunken fecklessness. She resents the 'respectability' the Ivolgins hang onto, denied to her, and both fears and yet courts their contempt. She unmasks the General, a habitual liar, by catching him out plagiarising a tall story from the newspapers – which involves his claiming to have insouciantly thrown a lady's lap-dog out of a train window, in revenge for the lady's having thrown out his cigar.

The second scandal occurs at Nastasya Filipovna's birthday party, where four men compete for her favours: Totsky, who is ceding his claim to Ganya; General Yepanchin, who has given her a pearl necklace; and Rogozhin, who had, in an earlier scene, bid 18,000, then 40,000 and finally 100,000 rubles for her. Nastasya becomes increasingly wild. She may indeed have gone mad during the scene itself. She momentarily chooses the Prince, who is the only man to love her disinterestedly, and who, we discover, is to inherit a fortune himself. Then she takes Rogozhin's 100,000 rubles and throws them on the fire, to taunt the greedy Ganya, who blenches and trembles at this treatment. Then she runs off with Rogozhin.

It is hard to convey, in any bald account of the plot, the feverish excitement of such scenes, and how convincingly Dostoevsky evokes the deep chaos inside the human mind. He shows how, in moments of high emotion, his characters act out roles that are incomprehensible even to themselves, and does all this with an art that is immediate, accidental in feeling, open-ended and absurd; and which yet convinces us that things could not easily have been otherwise. No other writer can so well convey the necessary, dizzy-making incompleteness of all moment-to-moment experience.

Each of the four parts revolves around one such major scandal; there are minor ones too. In part II the chief scandal concerns the irruption of Burdovsky, falsely claiming to be the proper heir to Myshkin's fortune, with his band of young nihilists, who, besides trying to extort money from the Prince, provide the audience to a defamatory letter about the Prince written to the newspaper by Keller and Lebedev. In part III comes the dying Ippolit's reading of his confession; and part IV gives us the Prince and Aglaya's engagement party, at which the Prince offends by speechifying against Catholicism, having an epileptic fit, and breaking a valuable Chinese vase.

The problem for any critic of Dostoevsky is how it can be that the most ideological of novelists should be, by some paradox, the most open-ended of writers to read, who has generated the most diverse disputes as to his meaning. The role of comedy is crucial here, hospitable as it is to Dostoevsky's interest in doubleness and self-contradiction. The power of the story, moreover, often springs from the dialogue, always acutely rendered. Dostoevsky at his best involuntarily loses himself in the distinctive speech patterns of his characters. Without the theatricality of extended dialogue, his scenes can stay merely melodramatic – for example the silent scene in part II in which

Rogozhin dogs the Prince and tries to knife him. And at his most 'rational', Dostoevsky can be engagingly childish, as in the advice as to how unoriginal but ambitious men may suffer from serious liver complaints (IV.1); or in the curious beauty tips to middle-aged ladies in *Crime and Punishment* (III.1), where a 'pure and sincere warmth of heart' is said to be particularly efficacious. Where he identifies with his characters and sacrifices his own prophetic impulses, he is most persuasive. Where he intrudes and ventriloquises, as in Myshkin's diatribe against Catholicism in part IV, the result can be doubly embarrassing.

The character of Myshkin increasingly intrigued and puzzled his own creator, and his best characters are all both inhabited and yet enigmatic. He gives us no single code to read by, rather some disparate clues. The improbable often discloses the real, he tells us, through Lebedev (III.4). The solution to one mystery may take the form of a new, more painful mystery (IV.8). And he is in any case concerned to present, he twice tells us, not an analysis of motivation, which is infinitely complex and obscure, however much we adore to rationalise it later, but a chronicle of events (IV.3, 8). What we have is not wholly indeterminate either, and, when, towards the magnificent and tragic end of the book, the devious narrator pretends to abdicate to allow 'Rumour' (IV.9) to take over the plot, we are given a travesty of truthfulness which we have by now been sufficiently schooled to recognise as such.[10]

* * *

Before turning to comedy, some account of what the comic has to engage with is necessary. It is certainly a squalid and raw-enough world, the world Prince Myshkin has been invented to display compassion in, and for – a world of 'trollops, generals, usurers' (I.12). Nastasya has been used and is now sold to the highest bidder. And here all emotions are corrupted by the market-place. The young nihilists who descend in part II have a cannibalistic individualism, concerned to extort and slander, to claim their 'rights' at any cost. A recurrent theme, related by Lebedev to *Revelations*, predicts the end of the world in a general reduction of all human relations to the demand for 'rights', shorn of pity, faith or any human regard. Ganya Ivolgin, 'wicked, rapacious, impatient, envious, and, in a word,

inordinately selfish' (1.4), marrying for money, with his scheming
sister who marries the usurer Ptitsyn, and his drunken liar of a
father, represents one centre of selfish vulgarity in the novel;
the treacherous Lebedev, with his meaningless parroting of
'I'm vile, I'm vile', is another. Yet the struggling Ivolgins
merely display nakedly the ruling passion for money and
position that, in the Yepanchins, is somewhat hidden by
success. General Yepanchin is secretly another greedy citizen,
rich, yet money-minded.

The apocalyptic and prophetic themes, moreover, are worked
out in some detail. There are many discussions of last moments,
and a pervasive rhetoric of 'the penultimate'. The Prince has
two digressions on execution in part 1 – might a decapitated
head go on thinking for a few moments? he ponders. Lebedev
has a piteous, absurd private cult of the Countess Du Barry, for
her sad end on the guillotine. The Prince suffers two epileptic
fits, with their accompanying sense of an ending, their auras of
apocalyptic terror or joy, one of them precipitated by Rogozhin's
attempt to knife him. Ippolit's 'Confession' is enlivened by the
fact that he has only weeks to live, and further helped on by his
announcing that he plans to kill himself as soon as he stops
reading. Nastasya, too, courts her own destruction, and the
entire book, once we finish reading, seems to have occurred
during a brief interval before the Prince's final descent into
madness. Numerous small tales and narratives concern real,
contemporary crime, faith, and unbelief, and eschatological
terrors – for example, Ippolit's account of the Holbein *Deposition*
that hangs in reproduction in Rogozhin's gloomy house. The
cruel details of physical torment on Christ's body negate, for
him, any possibility of resurrection, and the Prince, too,
comments that such a picture could destroy an onlooker's faith.
There is no doubt that Dostoevsky depicts the modern age as
under the seal of doom.

And yet, against these crisis ethics that so appeal to the modern
critic, another reading is possible, that emphasises the human,
intimate, provisional and comic genius of Dostoevsky, and
Myshkin's role as impresario of comic effects. If Myshkin is
double, both idiot and saint, so is his story both tragedy and
comedy. Hingley tells us that the idea that Myshkin represents
a serious ethical ideal is 'perhaps the richest piece of comedy
about him' (1962, p. 111) – as if the comic must always

undercut the serious. This cannot be so. It is not merely that the comedy stands *in opposition to* the sentimentality of darkness, though it can, but that it can also be one vehicle for Dostoevsky's serious purpose. In a marvellous passage in *The Diary of a Writer*, Dostoevsky speaks of the problem of describing a scene of painful squalor, adding, 'One could express even here a great deal of humour, and it would be very much to the point; *for humour is the wit of deep feeling.* I very much like this definition of it' (March 1877, III.2 cited in Peace, 1971, p. 330). Along with the harshly irreverent glee that Dostoevsky both criticises and expresses, and his pleasure in cruelty, grotesquerie and *Grand Guignol*, there is also a comedy of proportion and a humour that comes from a sane and cheerful focusing of disorder: the 'wit of deep feeling'.

The critic Bakhtin gets closest to seeing this; his superb point about Myshkin is that he has the function of destroying the *false seriousness* that disunifies life and divides people (Bakhtin, 1984, p. 174). The scandals that mark this novel more than most are thus treated by Bakhtin as anarchic episodes of 'carnival'. Here artificial divisions are broken down, 'dignity' is painfully surrendered, authority is therapeutically mocked, and a festive indeterminacy and more inclusive sense of community rule over all.

If he attacks 'false seriousness', Myshkin does this also by calming people down and by cheering them up. He puts their fears about indignity to rest, showing what it is to live without an anxious egoism. Neither talent is negligible or common, both often misfire in the book, and both are related to the comic in that comedy, too, at its best, penetrates our self-importance and relaxes our sense of painful separateness. We need not choose, in the scenes of scandal, between the comedy of indignity or the sheer pain: we are granted both inside and outside views of the action, undergo the ugly distress and enjoy the farce. The comedy is not opposed to the moral point but can (sometimes) be its best friend and essential vehicle. To have a good will in a bad world – as the hero of Dostoevsky's 'The Dream of a Ridiculous Man' discovers – is to be necessarily absurd. And, if Myshkin, instead of calming people down, on occasion arouses their intense indignation, this too has its funny side. He does not always, or finally, succeed.

As he early notes, Myshkin is 'a complete child' (I.6). In the

railway carriage he is guileless in his answers to Rogozhin,
lacking ordinary concern for his own privacy. He discusses his
ignorance of women, his illness and the intimate details of his
life as if he lacked that strong sense of owning an inner self that
typifies the others. As Rogozhin sees, he is a holy fool – 'and such
as you God loves' (I.1). He is given to making long speeches
on subjects of burning interest to himself, regardless of context –
on guillotining to the Yepanchin footman, on a mock execution
to the Yepanchin women, on the execrability of Catholicism at
his engagement party. These are curious topics to launch into
within minutes of meeting total strangers. He is outside ordinary
logic, too, in his belief that he can love two women at once, and
that he can show brotherly love for his murderously jealous
rival Rogozhin. Yet, when not disconnected from the moment
or making rhetorical gestures, he is preternaturally attentive,
and has the gift of emotional immediacy. He can read minds
and faces, and intuit their essential suffering – as when, on first
being shown Nastasya's photograph, he divines her suffering,
her pride and even the possibility (reiterated later) that
Rogozhin, if married to her, might murder her with a knife a
week later (I.3, II.3). On meeting the Yepanchin women he is
partly the intuitive knower who understands everyone that he
meets, partly the wise teacher who knows the secret of happiness.
'You're a philosopher and you've come to instruct us', says
Aglaya (I.5).

Shestov noted that the Christian doctrine of passive resistance
to evil is found 'the most terrible . . . irrational . . . and
mysterious' doctrine in the Gospels.[11] Myshkin embodies this
smireniye (humility or submissiveness), though not to the point
where he lacks all moral vigour. He tells Ganya the truth about
the latter's marriage plans: 'shameful' (I.11), and then provokes
him further by analysing, with a cruel spontaneity, his
unremarkable, ambitious personality. He stuns Nastasya, too,
by his simplicity and directness in seeing through her special
hypocrisy of always needing to portray herself as worse than
she really is. ' "And aren't you ashamed of yourself?" cried the
Prince with deep, heart-felt reproach, "You're not the woman
you pretend to be. Why, it isn't possible!" ', to which she
whispers, flushing violently, 'He was right . . . I'm not really
like that' (I.10). As Ganya puts it, 'You notice things other

people never notice. One could have a real talk with you, though, perhaps, one had better not' (I.11)!

Myshkin is present at almost every major scene in the book; but his difference from the other characters is plainest in the ugly, funny scenes of scandal. These are forcing-houses for the plot, speeding it on, and sharing common features. They often start with the unheralded arrival of a drunken mob – in this book, champagne being the favourite tipple. They are sometimes forecast, like the weather – 'Scandalous incidents . . . may well happen . . . before this evening' (I.3). The presence of an audience acts as echo-chamber, or burning-glass, to the high, theatrical emotions that are let loose. Beginning with a roll-call of those present,[12] the scandal scenes end in the painful, public destruction of the protagonists' sense of privacy. A feast of indignity results, disturbing most characters' peace of mind. Most Dostoevsky characters are easily bruised; few resist the temptation to take out their hurt on someone else. The exception is the Prince, who absorbs pain without spreading it around and without defending himself. At the opposite extreme is Ganya, among the swiftest to collect grievances and nurse resentments, and the least forgiving, though the Prince wins even him over. He slaps the Prince in frustration in part I, but, as the Prince predicts, is later ashamed and begs forgiveness. Many of the characters are caught up in some terrible machine of guilt, pain and vengefulness, and the scandals release these ruthless emotions, bruising the separate sense of self of the protagonists, who are humbled into membership – often unavowed or resisted – of the general community-in-sin. Myshkin shows the way, which not all are able to follow. To say this is to point out that the novel comprises only fools and holy fools, and the scandals are powerful scenes of communal foolery in which everyone plays the fool. Myshkin, as clown of God, shows the others how to be less fiercely attached to their own sense of dignity, and hence he is at once the butt of and chorus to the book's laughter.

He spends much of the book laughing, often joining in laughter at his own expense, never at the expense of others. 'People can't help laughing at me', he announces, to Aglaya's fury (III.2), and the narrator comments ironically at Myshkin's reappearance at the start of part II that his unworldly way of

wearing new clothes might cause anyone so disposed at least
to smile. The Prince is silent, however, when the company jeer
at Lebedev (III.4), but laughs loudly after being deeply shamed
at General Ivolgin's outrageous lies about having been
Napoleon's page in 1812 (IV.5), laughs 'with the utmost good
humour' at Lebedev's horrible intrigues (IV.3), laughs at
Aglaya's inscrutable gift of a hedgehog (IV.5). When others
approach him with ulterior motives, and then acknowledge the
fact, as often happens, that too makes him laugh. Thus he
laughs when agreeing with Radomsky that the latter may well
wish to cheat him or gain some advantage over him (III.4); and,
when Keller purports to confess his wicked actions, but in fact
claims his own acts with opportunistic pride – he seeks to soften
Myshkin and gain money from him – the two end up 'laughing
like madmen' together (II.11). Finally he laughs crazily during
the scene of the vase-breaking (IV.7), and laughs sympathetically
when he comforts Nastasya at the end before her murder: 'He
laughed when she laughed, cried when she cried' (IV.8). Thus
he cuts through the 'false seriousness' of the world. It is a
crucial part of the novel's deep wit that Myshkin's lack of an
exaggerated sense of self should sometimes aggravate the others.
To watch someone lacking in the sense of self-preservation is
disturbing if your own sense of where your advantage lies is
highly developed. And this opportunism the others naturally
possess.

Myshkin's presence in the book cuts through the reader's
'false seriousness' too, and softens the act of judgement we
make as we read. Even the poisonous Lebedev, symbol of social
corruption, is as much clown as villain. He is drunkard, lecher,
hypocrite. He cruelly taunts the pitiful General Ivolgin, and
repeatedly betrays Myshkin, both in helping write the
defamatory letter of part II, and finally in trying, before the fact,
to get him committed as insane after he abandons Aglaya for
Nastasya in part IV. Yet, we are told (through the Prince), he
probably adores his odious nephew, who is emotionally
blackmailing him (II.5); he is shown capable of hurt jealousy in
his relations with the Prince (IV.3), and sheds 'real tears' over
General Ivolgin at exactly the point when he has helped
torment him to death (IV.6). What is so striking about the
terrible load of guilt that Dostoevsky's characters always bear is
the wonderful innocence with which they bear it: so that

Dostoevsky does not scorn to use Lebedev, too, as a moral mouthpiece at times, for his views on the approaching apocalypse or on the emptiness of a life without faith (iii.4). The characters of *The Idiot* have the heedless malice and awesome destructiveness of small children; but also their innocence. It is hard to explore either aspect without appearing to underplay the other. Although Bakhtin makes little of the load of individual suffering and sin the characters bear, the manner of his neglect gets closer to the book's truth than those critics who, like Mrs Yepanchin, fussily 'magnify misfortune' (iii.1), because it is closer to the side of Dostoevsky that revels in the irreducibility – and actuality – of his own characters.

This particular vision seems richer than that of *Crime and Punishment*, by the disorderly size of its canvas, the ripeness of its comedy, and the inclusiveness of its moral vision. Ippolit in his ludicrous, horrible confession sees himself, unlike the gnat dancing in the sunlight, as an outcast from the 'banquet and chorus of life', and Myshkin sadly recognises Ippolit's lonely pain, his illusion that only he feels alone, while everything else in the world 'has its path and knows its path; it departs with a song and it comes back with a song' (iii.7). Banquet, chorus, dance and song: these are images of celebration, as well as of exclusion. 'Are you happy?' is a question repeatedly put in this novel – by Nastasya to Myshkin (iii.10), by Aglaya to Myshkin (i.5), by Myshkin to Aglaya (ii.1). Dostoevsky's characters are perhaps never happy with the spectacular innocence of Tolstoi's, or the wistful pain of Turgenev's; yet there is a fierce joy in this book which cohabits with much blackness. When the dying Ippolit asks the wise Myshkin what would be the best – i.e. most virtuous – way for him to die, Myshkin replies, 'Pass by us, and forgive us our happiness' (iv.5), a speech E. H. Carr rightly calls one of the great answers in literature (1931, p. 217). 'Ha, ha, ha! I thought so! I certainly expected something of the kind!' replies Ippolit, ending the chapter with a fierce mockery that cannot cancel out the eloquence it has invited, but joins even the 'highest' eloquence to a carnival mockery.

In such a celebration of opposites, emotions repeatedly collide or collude with their contraries. 'How could such a genuine and beautiful feeling be combined with such obvious and malicious mockery?' asks the Prince, of Aglaya's reading of the Pushkin poem that enshrines her own hunger for an ethical ideal, and also her wishful identification of Myshkin with that ideal (II.7). The formal answer to his question seems to be that, again and again, comedy enshrines and safeguards this complexity of feeling. Spite is comically dogged by altrium, magnanimity haunted by malice. Varya feels venomously at times towards her brother Ganya, but she none the less loves him 'sincerely and compassionately' (IV.4). Ippolit lets the Prince in on the secret of the meeting of his two loves, Nastasya and Aglaya, 'out of spite, not magnanimity' (IV.8), as he insists, but the two emotions are hard to tease apart here. When Mrs Yepanchin 'kindly' sees Myshkin off the premises after his disastrous breaking of the vase in part IV, telling him he will always remain a friend of the family, Dostoevsky comments how much cruelty there was hidden inside her eagerness to find something kind and heartening to say (IV.8), and our assent here is like a healing surrender to the multiplicity of life itself. As Ippolit says, in the middle of his terrible scene with Mrs Yepanchin in part II, 'You're kind, and the Prince, too, is kind – we're all quite absurdly kind people' (ch. 9) – before a further mutual outburst of cruelty and anger.

The sense of the characters' innocence is connected with their being partly seen as children. 'It is through children that the soul is cured', the Prince early comments (I.6), and the novel – like *The Brothers Karamazov*, reads at times like a sermon on Matthew 18:3: 'Except ye . . . become as little children, ye shall not enter the kingdom of heaven.' The 'originality' Dostoevsky praises at the start of part III is not that which comes from straining after effect, like Ferdyschenko, or from vanity and scheming, like Ganya, but that which accompanies the noble unselfishness of the child, such as Kolya Ivolgin possesses, though there are signs that he may lose it as he develops later into 'a very practical man of affairs' (Conclusion). Both Myshkin and Mrs Yepanchin are not only seen as children themselves, but see others so. 'Wicked boys . . . impertinent boys . . . horrible boys' (II.12, III.1), Mrs Yepanchin variously typifies – and thus humanises – the nihilists of part II. Children are attracted to Myshkin throughout, from the Swiss children in his story of Marie in part I, to Kolya, who is divided between the negations of Ippolit (himself only seventeen) and Myshkin. To Aglaya's anger, Myshkin uses schoolboy slang (IV.6); and he sees Nastasya, too, as 'a child, an absolute child' (IV.9). This

habit of discerning the child behind others' guile is noted by
Keller. Keller has come to him, like so many characters, out of
a mixed desire to make use of him, and then finds himself
disarmed into deeper candour. Seeing only the best in all he
meets, the Prince tells Keller that his is a trusting, child-like
and extraordinarily truthful nature (ii.11) and encourages him
by remarking how terribly difficult it is to fight against 'these
double thoughts'. Keller had acknowledged his continuing desire
to get money from the Prince at the very moment that he felt
melted with contrition – and this further admission is then, of
course, used as a moral bribe to the Prince. Keller lowers his
requirements, however, from 150 to 25 rubles, as a result!
Moved by the glimpse Myshkin gives him of his own potential
goodness, he retorts, 'Oh, Prince, how utterly in the Swiss
manner, so to speak, you understand human nature', implying
that Myshkin's gift is to see, like Rousseau, only the original
innocence of the human heart, a capacity Keller at first sees as
a damaging liability. It is, indeed, a real question as to how far
Myshkin's short-sightedness with evil in the end disequips him
in his dealings with others and contributes to our final sense
that he has little place in this world.

Mrs Yepanchin, however, in this world of adults-seen-as-
children, has a prime place. For all her abruptness, intensity
and combative inconsequence, her guilelessness, too, is a
constant source of delight. Dostoevsky has a special affection
for and expertise in creating foolish, middle-aged ladies of
bourgeois or noble extraction. In this he resembles Dickens. His
depth of portraiture, with Mrs Raskolnikov, Mrs Stavrogin
and, here, Mrs Yepanchin, seems to me greater. He excels at
the type of the bustling, foolish emotionally intense matriarch,
and Mrs Yepanchin is one of his finest creations. She has an
irresistible temper that does battle with a warm heart, and an
unshakable conviction that she has *very effective eyes* (i.5). Kolya,
Ippolit and Myshkin all see that she is at heart as simple as a
child. She dramatises each situation that occurs, alternates
between being conciliatory and querulous, and dominates her
bien-pensant, foolish, money-minded husband. Morbidly touchy –
a general Dostoevskian characteristic – she is also noble and
kind-hearted, as Myshkin sees. Some of her folly relates to her
want of education – she embarrasses her daughters by failing to
recognise the Pushkin poem Aglaya recites; but she is also

hysterical and peremptory. 'I want to hear that poem *at once*', she tells the company, and then demands a copy of it. Her idiotic vehemence can precipitate distress – as when she insists on the public reading of the newspaper libel on the Prince – and she also has a habit of 'exploding like a bomb' (III.1). Some of her frustration comes from a sense of being excluded from her three beloved and 'modern' daughters' lives, and from a baffled desire to protect and control. The generation gap is clearly delineated: the 'woman question' is constantly in the air. She fears that Aglaya may have cut off her beautiful hair because she is a nihilist: she fears her *modernity*.

Dostoevsky is always a keen observer of human *argument*. In this novel we have Aglaya nearly quarrelling with Prince Sh. because he fails to find the position of a particular park bench remarkable; Mrs Yepanchin's anger with Alexandra because the latter has a dream of *nine geese*; and the quarrels of Mrs Yepanchin and Kolya. 'The first time they quarrelled over the "woman question" and the second time *over the best season in the year for catching siskins*' (II.1; emphasis added). Their sparring hides real affection, and our delight here comes from Dostoevsky's showing us the depth, as well as the absurdity, of human irritability – partly through the way the 'innocence' of the second topic (siskin-catching) itself argues with the momentousness of the first (feminism). Both Kolya and she are children. When she charges herself with being a silly, ill-mannered, eccentric old woman, whose eccentricities will keep possible suitors to her daughters at bay, Dostoevsky values her 'originality' as she does not herself. With the Prince, whom she at once adopts, she is moved alternately to violent indignation and to pity. And she weeps bitter and generous tears when events have again finally reduced him to lunacy, and is given the last word on the corruptions and inconveniences of the Western Europe in which he is now incarcerated for good.

With young and dying Ippolit (either seventeen or eighteen, the text is unclear), Mrs Yepanchin veers between fury at his insolent, godless defiance, and heartfelt compassion at his imminent death from TB. Radomsky had argued that self-preservation is by no means the only natural law under which mankind labours: other emotions, darker and more self-destructive, also obtain (III.4), and each can be felt in Ippolit's case. He first appears among the group of adolescent nihilists tormenting the Prince in Book Two, but soon after takes a central place in the story. He holds court in Book Three to read his so-called 'Necessary Explanation', a bizarre mixture of purported autobiography, dream, and callow philosophising. His voice is described as squeaking 'unnaturally' and screaming 'shrilly'. His stagey performance angers his hearers. He is frozen in a state of adolescent combat with the world, and wants a reaction from it that will confirm his own significance, and will attenuate the bitter sting of having to die so young and untried. The Prince says that Ippolit wants the admiration of the world, to bless and be blessed (iii.8). At the same time he is an 'underground man' whose confession is a species of attack or revenge upon his hearers. He purports to speak the 'naked truth', 'nothing but the truth', but this recalls the bogus 'Truth-game' played in part i: those in Dostoevsky who live without faith also live outside the truth, and, no matter how strenuously they pursue it, are always finally cheated of it. If there are some deep truths Ippolit is privy to, there are others he is excluded from understanding, by virtue of his anger, spite, pain and fury with a world that will not confirm his genius, and in which he is unsure whether he has been vouchsafed any remarkable gifts in the first place.

And yet, Ippolit is simultaneously one of the demonic characters through whom Dostoevsky gives vent to his own doubts, testing his own pieties – in an intensely and recognisably 'modern' spirit – to breaking-point. His performance is prefaced by Lebedev's apocalyptic warnings about modern faithlessness, interspersed with spiteful taunts and challenges to his hearers, and pretentiously epigraphed, 'Après moi, le deluge'. He recounts a nightmare in which a terrified dog bites in two a repulsive, surreal scorpion-like 'reptile', stinging itself and cracking white fluid from the shell. The dream presents social relations as warfare, and seems also to dramatise the fight between 'self-preservation' and 'self-destruction', the two equally ruthless dark powers whose embattlement Radomsky had earlier noted. Ippolit is allowed, like the Underground Man, Dostoevsky's own emphasis on life as a process of continuing discovery, without any final goal or safety. He then tells a self-flattering and 'literary' tale of his having assisted a destitute family, and, having impersonated an altruist and developed a heroic self-image, he now impersonates a tyrant in his relations with his casual hearers. He may yearn for love, but behaves in such a way as to make it difficult for most people to give him any. He defies any theodicy, picturing God as a 'huge and horrible tarantula', a dark, deaf-and-dumb, all-powerful creature; ponders the irony that, if he were now to turn murderer, he might die in comfort in a prison hospital, his illness indemnifying him against worse punishment. The one act of defiant 'free will' left to him is suicide. He now mounts this suicide with more stage heroics, spoiling the final effort by failing properly to load his pistol. Radomsky, who despises these histrionics, none the less fears sleepless nights as a result of witnessing them, and the contemporary reader, too, is haunted and disturbed by Ippolit's relentless hatred, his tormented egoism and his detailed spite. He has already been shown to us as a person who avenges himself on his audience for witnessing his weaknesses, becoming particularly spiteful after having sobbed like a child in the scene of the nihilists' slanders. He is likewise, on the whole, more malevolent after his humiliating attempted suicide than before. He lives on to denounce Ganya, who shares his 'mediocrity', and who is angry with him for, among other reasons, failing to die on time, 'as he had promised'. He dies at the last in terrible agitation.

Myshkin can only offer Ippolit comfort; he cannot save him from himself. With General Ivolgin he is, at moments, more successful. In part IV General Ivolgin has stolen 400 rubles from Lebedev to pay for his drinking, and then attempted, to avoid open scandal, to return the wallet and money. He puts it back under his chair, where Lebedev, to torment him, refuses to see it. He then puts it back into the lining of his coat. Lebedev is playing a dangerous game with the General, who is a drunken liar and a failure. There is literally 'no truth' in him. He lies, automatically, instinctively, pointlessly, and also comically. Unlike Lebedev's own opportunistic lies, the General's profit no one. He tells small spur-of-the-moment lies – such as that he knows Nastasya's flat well and will direct the Prince to it; habitual *canards*, such as that he has heard his horse talk; and pieces of sentimental *blague*, when he meets those younger than himself, that he 'held them in his arms as a child'. When he tries this out on Aglaya in part I, he finds, to his shocked surprise, that he has inadvertently told the truth, *by mistake*, and experiences a rush of memory, a sense of squandered chances and of present disgrace, that moves him to real and not crocodile tears. It is a moment of great humour and pathos. The General has lived for so long in a world of fantasy to protect his few remaining shreds of self-respect that he has in effect lost contact with the real world. His preposterous boasts – like Ippolit's spite – are designed as ointment to his injured vanity; but they provide a backwash of doubt which can only be countered by a further indulgence, to the excruciating distress of his family.

Lebedev is up to a dangerous game in trying to show the General to himself. He toys with the General's lying as well as with his thieving, inventing a cock-and-bull story of having had his leg shot off and buried with a farcical inscription, which provokes the General to the sustained invention of having been Napoleon's page during the 1812 campaign, and of having been personally responsible for the retreat. The old General appeals to the Prince with the plea that he'd like to be able to respect himself. 'A man with so noble an ambition is worthy of respect on that account alone' (IV.3): the Prince delivers this somewhat specious, copybook phrase and finds that it flatters, soothes, touches and pleases the old man, who, deeply moved, starts an incomprehensible rigmarole that at least indicates that he has been comforted and strengthened. He none the less suffers a stroke and dies.

Myshkin is more interesting as a moral agent than as a theorist, however fallible he is in both roles. To see him, as have some critics, as solitary redeemer involved in a failed attempt at the Second Coming is to put an intolerable strain on him, even when we are reminded that Christ, too, was a failure. This is the critic's version of what Bakhtin termed 'false seriousness'. It is Myshkin's human, fallible quality that keeps him interesting. And Dostoevsky builds in his own caveats against the prophetic impulse. He makes Lebedev excuse his own cruel taunting of General Ivolgin by arguing that 'Everybody has his worries, Prince, especially in our strange and turbulent age' (IV.3). The sense that some large historical force is acting through one, or that one passively embodies such a force, is a uniquely *modern* kind of corrupt justification. The novel's judgement works, on the whole, against such an irresponsible 'prophetic' historicism, in favour of a more localised view of truth.

Murray Krieger has argued that Myshkin's effect is, none the less, little short of disastrous, and that he drives the others to distraction through forgiving them. Throughout the tale, the more his interlocutors rage over their lack of control over their own lives, the more affronted they are by the Prince's undefended open heart. It is as if his emptiness and meekness threatened their more grasping mode of being, by offering a tacit judgement on it, a judgement the more abrasive for being one of which Myshkin is wholly unconscious. On the contrary, it is they who are puritanically judgemental and censorious, while he is maddeningly forgiving. In such ways his *dictum* that 'meekness is a terrific force' (III.6) has purchase. Krieger, however, argues that Myshkin's power repeatedly *drives* the others to regrettable actions.[13] This is a condescending argument. Characters so lacking in moral will themselves that they require the excuse of being 'forgiven by Myshkin' to justify stupid and self-destructive actions will be neither very interesting nor very self-determined to begin with.

Myshkin's relations with the two girls are, to say the least, none the less odd. Originally Dostoevsky intended Myshkin–Rogozhin as another of his 'double' characters. The separation of Rogozhin, the demonic, passionate half, has the effect that the two characters still feel strangely comfortable together when they meet. But it also leaves Myshkin insufficiently *fleshly*. At times he occupies a different metaphysical realm from the other characters, and Dostoevsky's hesitation about the Prince's human/spiritual status becomes troublesome once he is engaged to be married. Myshkin twice volunteers the information that he is ignorant of women, either virginal or impotent (I,1, 3). What business, we may justly feel, has he with marriage.

An effective saint might be expected to show both an uncompromising detachment form the world and yet an accurate intuition about the laws which govern its workings. Myshkin acquires the latter too slowly not to be overtaken by events. Without worldly wisdom, his altruism is not always skilfully deployed. He is as naïve about money – being over-generous to his creditors (at first) – as he is about love. And the qualities that attract Nastasya to him are also those that prevent him from keeping her. He feels compassion for her and mistakes this for love. Throughout the tale, pity is the chief kind of love he recognises.

At one level Nastasya is a stagy conception, the fallen woman

who is mad, bad and dangerous to know. Dostoevsky
triumphantly makes her staginess the key to her personality:
she is *acting out* her role and it is a theatrical performance. She
repeatedly and publicly boasts that she is a 'street-walker', a
'shameless slut' (i.16), who will 'go on the streets'. She knocks
Myshkin out of the way when she first sees him, though she is
normally kind to servants, and is probably more chaste than
she wishes the world to think. 'Am I a loose woman? Ask
Rogozhin, he'll tell you!' (iv.8), she tells Aglaya. Her relationship
with Keller, like others of the riotous circle who provide her
with a court, and who is briefly chosen as favourite, is also
chaste.

Myshkin understands that she has internalised all the blame
for her seduction by Totsky, as violated children are said to do,
and is maddened by it. She is living out a life-myth of depravity,
whose falseness Myshkin astonishes her by unmasking at once.
His faith in her maintains a new self-image by which she is
beguiled but with which she cannot fully identify. Since she can
neither forgive herself, nor wholeheartedly accept the Prince's
forgiveness, she opts for further punishment to procure at least
the potent pleasure of humiliation. This is a demonic parody of
Myshkin's true meekness, of course, just as Lebedev travesties
humility by aping it as masochism. Nastasya swings between
Rogozhin and Myshkin – too good for the first, too bad, as she
thinks, for the latter. Deciding that she is not good enough for
the Prince and will disgrace him, she simultaneously decides
that Aglaya is right, developing a fantasy relation with her,
writing letters to her, half falling in love with her – falling in
love, as it were, with an idealised notion of her own lost 'pure'
self, and staging two minor scandals to discredit Radomsky, a
rival for Aglaya's hand, to release Aglaya for the Prince.

The meeting between the two women in part iv is a
magnificent scene, histrionic as the expression of intense emotion
can be, and very painful indeed. Aglaya is determined to cut
through Nastasya's pretences, and the result is a jealous duel, a
cat-fight involving increasing exchange of malice and insult.
Aglaya accuses her of being a bookish woman who has never
done a stroke of work in her life, and who loves her own
humiliation. 'If you wanted to be an honest woman, why didn't
you give up your seducer Totsky simply, without any theatrical
scenes?' (iv.8), she asks, and, partly to repay Aglaya back for

having thus hurt her, partly as a demonstration of power, Nastasya reclaims the Prince despite his engagement to Aglaya.

Because he pities Nastasya more, he hesitates between them – fatally, so far as Aglaya is concerned. She leaves without him, and the Prince and Nastasya are to be married – except that, at the last moment of course, Nastasya once again sees the passionately jealous Rogozhin and flies off with him, to her death. Rogozhin had earlier told the Prince that 'she is marrying me *to die*' (ii.3), to have her guilt assuaged and her pain rewarded. When left alone with Nastasya he comforts her as one would a child, absorbed in her distress and apparently blandly forgetful of Aglaya's.

As for Aglaya, she marries a fraudulent Polish 'count' and converts to Catholicism, a religion and a national cause that Dostoevsky abhorred. Is Myshkin responsible? A little. But Aglaya is also her mother's daughter, with her Romantic idealism, her impatient refusal of reality, her peevish contrariness and her foot-stamping rages, and her persistent habit of saying one thing and meaning the opposite. She wishes to run away and do something useful with her life. She wants to be more than just a 'General's daughter'. She is passionate, contrary, and touchingly vulnerable. Krieger blames her fate on the Prince, but it is worth recalling that her mother typifies her fearfully as 'a headstrong girl, a fantastic girl, a crazy girl' (iii.8), and is constantly worried that she is hatching some self-destructive plan. The plot justifies Mrs Yepanchin's fears, too.

So, in the astonishing and powerful ending, the Prince and Rogozhin lie together on the makeshift bed, while Nastasya's figure, after her energy has filled the tale, lies in a horrifying immobility. A fly's buzzing accentuates her stillness and there are other terrible details – the 'good American cloth' with which Rogozhin has covered her, the four uncorked bottles of Zhdanov disinfectant to counteract the smell. The Prince strokes Rogozhin's hair as the latter rages and mutters incoherently. In the morning Rogozhin is in a fever, and Myshkin an idiot once more, taken back to Schneider's Swiss sanatorium, this time for good.

Radomsky is given a final word, twice endorsed by the (unreliable) narrator. He accuses Myshkin of a *quixotic*, that is disproportionate, compassion for Nastasya, fed by various conventional literary styles of feeling. He charges him with having smashed to pieces a treasure, as if his clumsiness with the Chinese vase foreshadowed his abandonment of Aglaya. To this speech we give some rational, but not our full emotional, assent. Wasiolek has shown how, through all the reworkings of the tale, Radomsky appears in the guise of inadequate, cynical rationalist, glib, aimless – 'an aristocratic scoffer', Lebedev calls him (III.4) with the balance-sheet mind Dostoevsky loathed. Yet Dostoevsky also rewards him with the good Vera Lebedev, and makes him genuinely afflicted on the Prince's behalf. It is only, however, a hopelessly pragmatic and schematic mind, weighing moral worth by some statistic of help and harm, that would read the tally sheet of results as the measure of Myshkin's worth. . . . He could offer the world love, but he could not transform it. He could take upon himself the pain of the world, even if he could not still the rage that inflicted it.

(Wasiolek, 1969, p. 15)

5

The Devils (1871)

The Devils (sometimes translated as *The Possessed*) was written both as a political and as a religious novel. It addresses the debates of the 1860s – 'strong' versus 'weak' literary types, generational conflict, the new nihilism – but, unlike the simple opposition of Turgenev's *Fathers and Sons*, which it explicitly rebukes, it shows the guilt of the 1840s idealists in *fathering* the new generation of 1860s nihilists.

The most flawed of the great novels, *The Devils* has also the hardest plot to follow and to paraphrase. The action, like that of *The Idiot*, develops through successive scandals, rather than along conventional plot-lines. There are, moreover, at least two main centres of interest: Stepan Trofimovich Verkhovensky, the footling middle-aged liberal, and the young man he has long ago tutored, and for whose ideas he is inadvertently responsible, the demonic Nicholas Stavrogin. Where Turgenev showed these two generations engaged in warfare, Dostoevsky shows them intimate and complicit one with the other. Verkhovensky, the man of the 1840s, is directly responsible for the revolutionary antics of the group he so deplores, who want Stavrogin as their leader. Moreover, while everyone in the book is obsessed by Stavrogin and affected by what he does, we are never made privy to his thoughts. These features, together with a narrator who is himself a character, half in, half out of the story, and an ambiguous comic tone, help frustrate easy entry into the novel.

As serious political comment, moreover, the book is notable (and laughable) for its complete demonisation of the idea of progress. The only 'advance' it documents since the days of Lermontov is the growth of new and more terrible kinds of malice (1.5.8). As a religious novel it further perplexes by the lack of any positive standard or character who can stand up

against the new malice and the burgeoning evil and disorder
that accompany it.

The chapter 'At Tikhon's' was to have presented such an
ideal. Here Stavrogin confessed a possible rape (the evidence is
ambiguous) of a fourteen-year-old girl, and the good Bishop
Tikhon wrestled with him for his soul. Mochulsky has argued
(1971, p. 465) that the omission of 'At Tikhon's' hurts this 'vast
icon diptych' of a book, by leaving only its single, dark panel,
while John Jones splendidly suggests, on the contrary (1983,
passim), that Dostoevsky could promote his own dearest values
only by creeping up on their blind side, and that his art arouses
our longing for the settled and the normal and the beautiful
itself – arouses it without satisfying it, a frustration that makes
Dostoevsky seem still so contemporary a figure.

The narrator here unsettles us further by being half inside,
half outside the action, and by intermixing lucidity with
vagueness and inconsequential fuss about detail. In the first
chapter this narrator tells us that the liberal circle to which he
belongs, known as a hotbed of free-thinking, vice and atheism,
was in fact merely a centre for the most amiable, jolly, typically
Russian liberal chatter. Among the predictions they make for a
renewed Europe is one that the Pope will step down and adopt
the role of simple bishop. 'But then, "Russian higher liberalism"
always dismissed everything as *airily* as that' (1.1.9; emphasis
added). The words 'higher', 'noble', 'lofty' all emit signs of
decay here, as if they were radioactive. The comedy assists this
decay because it drives reader and characters hard into
the intractable, often ugly, particulars of a world which
'imagination', at its airiest, tipsiest, giddiest, is always ready
to dismiss. A liberal abstraction denatures the world; comedy
painfully reinvents it. Idealism is impatient with contingency;
comedy delights in it and feeds off it. Fantastic visions of future
harmony collide with the awfulness of the band of comrades
dreaming them up. Liputin, for example, who gloats ecstatically
at night over visions of a future phalanstery (1.2.3) is an
insignificant, sometimes abject, jealous husband, a coarse family
tyrant, miser and money-lender, who locks up the remnants of
meals and candle-ends. The novel presents no human being
bearing the slightest resemblance to the republic of peace and
goodness of which he airily dreams. Politics is reduced to
vanity, self-will, destructive fantasy and escapism. The only

'revolution' mentioned with favour is that which momentarily occurs in Stepan Verkhovensky's heart when it encounters real pain, suggesting that he might change from fool into wise man. His airy fantasy of a tearfully 'beautiful' reunion with his demon son Peter, whom he knows so little that he even fails to recognise him, and whom he has cheated out of real affection and inheritance, has been smashed by Peter's pitiless public unmasking of his father (1.5.7). But the moment of grief-born wisdom passes swiftly.

Comedy, however, is never wholly abandoned. Even in the epidemic of horrifying deaths with which the tale ends, the flavour of 'curiously evil comedy' (J. Jones, 1983, p. 247) or of 'ambivalent laughter' (Bakhtin, 1984) continues to discomfort us: hell itself might indeed be full of mirth, as Dostoevsky's darkest of all tales, *Bobok*, with its spitefully quarrelling graveyard of corpses, suggests.

Two related scenes at the heart of this novel capture the strangeness of its comedy, which helps make it so hard a book to find one's bearings in. 'Our town' are on their way to see the saintly half-wit Semyon Yakovievich, from whom they expect much fun. He has, after all, recently ordered the Jew Lyamshin to be driven out with a broom, and to have two large boiled potatoes thrown after him. On the way the cavalcade stop to look at a young suicide in a hotel, about nineteen and very good-looking. 'Our ladies had never seen a suicide' (II.5.2). The boy shot himself after a pleasure-seeking spree in which he squandered 400 rubles. They stare at the dead boy with eager curiosity, exchanging witticisms. The jester Lyamshin steals some grapes, and others try to follow his example. The full disquiet of this scene comes from the insolent and callous detachment with which the company sight-see at a private grief, the impious pleasure they take in it as 'pure spectacle', and the careful abdication of the narrator from strenuous judgement. It is left to one anonymous observer to blurt out the question of why people have suddenly started hanging and shooting themselves so frequently, as if they had become uprooted or the ground had given way under their feet. Indeed, there are two more suicides to come – three, if we include Stavrogin's insulted Matryosha in the banned chapter. But the scene's true weightlessness comes not from its artful 'placing' of the chain of self-destruction, but from how it acts out the very lack of ordinary moral gravity the observer describes. 'Our town' here share both in the indifference of Stavrogin and in the heartless curiosity of Peter Verkhovensky. The viewing of the suicide is immediately followed by the trip to the saint, who enacts the moral judgement we have felt cheated of, but with the uncanny arbitrariness of the Queen in *Alice in Wonderland*: the amount of sugar in your tea indicates the moral favour you have earned, while the company stare at Semyon with the same anaesthesia of the moral sense, 'through lorgnettes, pince-nez, *even opera-glasses*' (ii.5.2; emphasis added). When a pretentious society woman begs Semyon to address her, she is rewarded by the saint's crying, 'Kick her in the ——!', using an 'extremely indecent word', so that the company break into 'Homeric laughter'.

'Homeric' seems exactly right here. In book i of the *Iliad* even the gods themselves are not immune from helpless laughter, malice and indignity, and in *The Devils*, too, malice has its degrees, from Liputin's malicious cheerfulness (i.1.8) to the 'innocent malice' on show in 'our town', which leads, in the end, to the upside-down world of the fête in part iii, the greatest set-piece scandal Dostoevsky ever dreamt up, and the *mise-en-scène* for the novel's multiple crises and its terrible ending.

*   *   *

The book is divided into three parts. Stepan Verkhovensky figures at once, in the introduction. He is the book's father-figure and, in a story in which everyone – even Stavrogin – turns out to be marginal, its principal 'superfluous man'. The anonymous narrator is his confidant and, a master of irony, is both owlishly polite to Stepan Verkhovensky and full of a heartless 'sympathy' for his plight which astonishes us in the end by the way it leaves him undiminished. He is one of Dostoevsky's greatest portraits, and stands indeed among the greatest literary creations. The narrator's 'respect' for the 'nobility' of his friend – another double narrator to fit a double tale – recalls Mark Antony's reiteration of 'honourable' for the conspirators in *Julius Caesar*, which empties it of content. Yet here irony never exhausts respect. 'Poor old friend! Good old friend!' (ii.10.9). 'The man was dear to me' (iii.1.4).

Stepan Verkhovensky acts out the role of forgotten great

writer and political dissident. In the notebooks he is named as Granovsky, a Westernising liberal of the 1840s mentioned at the start of the novel, with Chaadyev, Belinsky and Herzen. He is living out a life-myth of 'vanished glory' – both literary and political – and likes to frighten himself with thoughts of the mutual danger he and the State represent to one another. His early notability, such as it was, was based on a thesis investigating why medieval Hanau (like himself) never fulfilled its promise. He later started a 'most profound' research into the causes of the 'extraordinary moral nobility' of certain knights; and a poetic drama in the 1830s, in Romanticism's first flush, intensely funny in the narrator's cruel description, with its singing insects, crooning minerals, curses, fairies, insights and 'lofty' humour. Once more the approach to the Ideal triggers savage irony.

Stepan Trofimovich is a vain, handsome, distinguished-looking man in his fifties. Neither of his marriages lasted long. His first wife gave birth to a son, Peter, whom he had farmed out to some aunts in the provinces. The failure of his early hopes led him to accept the post of tutor to the whimsical and despotic Mrs Stavrogin, whose son Nicholas he helped to educate and form. A forgotten man, he has turned into an effete, pompous, sententious and trivial *poseur*, his youthful enthusiasm dissipated in champagne, cards, depression ('civic grief'), and his literary talent idly spent on epigrams and letters. These letters display him as another ardent, 'airy' fantasist, seeking urgently to compel reality through daydream. He pretends to read De Tocqueville in the garden, but actually reads light romances. The 'Hurrah!' he gave at the Emancipation of the Serfs had been rehearsed for one hour, in front of the looking-glass. His nature is intense, yet superficial; he weeps frequently, feeling emotions easily, voiding them with rapidity, acting them out. He is also a vain and silly, idle, touchy, footling fusspot, a stagy fop in a red tie, a restless, over-refined, prissy fribble, a thoughtless, irresolute, callous egoist, who sold off his old serf Fedka into military service to cover a gambling-debt. Fedka returns to do much mischief. Lastly, he is a neurasthenic and a gossip, a pathetic 'old woman' who, for all his helpless effeminacy, is passionately heterosexual, indeed totally dependent on women, up to his very death, before which he finds a Gospel woman to be his special new friend.

Dostoevsky's delight in his creation is palpable, and he adds small touches throughout the book that astonish by their 'rightness', from his 'peculiar gloatingly obsequious humour' to his comic surprise at discovering the shape of his own life. Despite never having *willed* the matter, he has turned into a parasite and sentimental clown to Mrs Stavrogin. '*Je suis un* ordinary hanger-on *et rien de plus*' (1.1.7). His persistent use of French, however, distinguishes this 'nothing more' he feels he has become, and renders it more than nothing. As Marya Lebyatkin says when she arrives in Mrs Stavrogin's drawing-room, 'Oh, French, French! You can see at once it's high society!' (1.5.1). From his smallest foible to his worst vanity, he is knowable – which is not at all to say that Dostoevsky could easily exhaust his own own, and our, discoveries about him. He is made mysteriously alive by the glow of publicity in which he moves, while his son Peter is mysterious by virtue of his *unknowability*, like Stavrogin.

Mrs Stavrogin, the most tyrannical of all Dostoevsky's bustling matriarchs, has an insatiable need to control and an unappeased social appetite. (The appearance of the 'great' writer Karmazinov, a cruel portrait of Turgenev, drives her to frenzy.) The love–hate relationship between Mrs Stavrogin and Stepan Trofimovich, in a book full of such love–hate relations, is remarkable. 'There are strange friendships: two friends are almost ready to kill each other, they go on like that all their lives, and yet they cannot bring themselves to part' (1.1.3). The mixture of deep need and affection in the relationship, and equally bitter hatred, jealousy, resentment and exasperation, is made actual for us. A tall, bony woman with a yellow complexion and an exceedingly long, horsy face, Mrs Stavrogin takes in Stepan Verkhovensky to enhance her standing, to fuss over and scheme with and care for. She even designs all his clothes. When her estranged husband dies, a new note of falseness enters their relations. She resents Stepan's supposition that she is waiting for him to propose to her, and resents it with such force that she may indeed have hoped for such a proposal. Their sentimental friendship is frozen in a state of semi-hostility until she experiences a sudden, violent desire to marry him off to her ward Dasha. Perhaps some perverse generosity underlies this – a vicarious desire to see him provided for in his love-life – but, if so, this is vexed by her intention to accompany them on their honeymoon, though she has not yet decided this important matter. 'I tell you she's an angel of goodness', she screams furiously to Stepan (1.2.7); and to Dasha in her turn she screams. 'He *must* adore you!' (1.2.6). Here a quixotic 'airiness' becomes vertiginous. Stepan's son Peter is (rightly) to scoff at the bogus 'noble' self-sacrificing zeal this marriage represents; a zeal in any case given away by the fact that Mrs Stavrogin's other motive is to cover up for her son Nicholas's misdemeanours. He has had some sort of love-passage abroad with Dasha, which she fears may compromise his chances with the desirable heiress Lisa Tushin. She wants to marry Dasha off to release her son for Lisa. She feels a new longing for her son that dates from the time of his marked social success in Petersburg. What she does not know is that he is secretly married already.

Critics have tended to favour the marvellous Stepan Trofimovich and to slight the domineering Mrs Stavrogin. It may be worth recalling, therefore, how he tactlessly, needlessly hurts her by gossiping about her as 'my prosaic friend' (1.2.1), excluding her from any real mutuality, just as he refuses, we later learn, to let her see the books she has specially ordered for him, whose pages he has in any case left uncut. The friendship, in any case, has the solid opacity of real-life relationships, where the truth of events is always hard, later, to secure, even though the emotions involved have so continuing a cutting edge. When he is on his death-bed, and despite the fact that it was she who bullied him, so absurdly, into the courtship, she reveals that she was none the less passionately jealous when he prettified himself to woo Dasha.

*   *   *

Mrs Stavrogin feels that Stepan Verkhovensky is her creation, that she 'invented' him. In a less self-conscious manner Stavrogin is, in turn, Verkhovensky's creation and spiritual heir. Against Turgenev's view of a simple opposition between the generations, Dostoevsky shows their indebtedness. Where Stepan has the 'cheap quibbling free-thinking' of his generation of 1840s idealists (1.3.10), and also their Romantic daydreams, Stavrogin, to whom he has acted as tutor, has the ethical nullity that Dostoevsky fears may follow from this bad diet.

Stavrogin is the book's absent centre – the subject of gossip, speculation and rumour before he appears. This is not until the first of the book's major scandals, in his mother's drawing-room, one third of the way through the book, and after he has been falsely announced on the arrival of Stepan's son, Peter Verkhovensky. After his rake-hell reputation, he surprises us by being merely handsome, amiable and curiously absent. He is often obstinately silent and – increasingly – fastidiously unapproachable.

Our exclusion from Stavrogin's inner life is clearly deliberate on Dostoevsky's part. Our relationship with Stavrogin proceeds by a fearful guesswork. There are stories of wild riot, brutality to women and two duels, in one of which he maimed his opponent and in the other killed him, with a consequent reduction to the ranks. There are also three mysterious scandals, by which 'our town' feels insulted. In the first of these 'idiotic and puerile' incidents (1.2.2), an elderly notable remarks that no one can lead *him* by the nose, upon which Stavrogin seizes and drags him a few steps by his nose across the floor. In the second he publicly kisses Liputin's wife, when dancing with her, because he notices how pretty she is. In the third he bites the ear of the former governor. As with Hamlet, to whom he is likened, there is extensive debate about whether he is mad.

Hamlet is only one princely heir-apparent with whom he is compared. Stepan Verkhovensky consoles Mrs Stavrogin by comparing him with Prince Hal, whose riotous youth in Shakespeare's *Henry IV* preceded a stately, respectable maturity. Peter Verkhovensky, who believes that in Stavrogin's immense personal fascination and power he has found a figure-head for the Revolution, calls him Prince Ivan; and the saintly half-wit and cripple Marie Lebyatkin, whom he has secretly married for obscure reasons, shows signs of having seen through his posturing insensitivity when she compares him with the false pretender Grishka Otrepyev. He has also, however, a more direct literary precedent in Pechorin, a character in Lermontov's *A Hero of Our Time*, published at the start of the 1840s, Stepan's decade. Pechorin is the first 'strong' superfluous man in Russian literature. Insolently detached, indifferently bored, a man of unbounded strength and pitiless honesty, his passion for contradiction and rebellion fascinated and repelled a generation. Lermontov saw that the fascination of such Romantic types lies

halfway between literature and life, as the satire on the *poseur*
Grushnitsky, whom Pechorin destroys, shows. Grushnitsky's
ambition is to become the hero of a novel; Pechorin, on the
other hand, is already seen as such by the other characters.
Stavrogin shares with Pechorin his 'central' myth, his diabolical
isolation, his cynical disdain and boredom. He is repeatedly
shown yawning (e.g. II.1.3). He is more complex than Pechorin,
however, or than Turgenev's nihilist Bazarov in *Fathers and
Sons*, who also accepts no principles on trust simply because
they are generally respected. He is shown in a more living
tension than either, between the poles of good and evil that
perplex his nature. He 'indulges all vileness and is in love with
the good' (J. Jones, 1982, p. 279). Immense spiritual power is,
in him, rendered sterile and corrupt through absence of moral
aim or purpose. He is one variant on the theme of the 'Great
Sinner', about which Dostoevsky at this time reflected much.
For those without faith, caprices and perversities of the will are
what remain.

One such perversity has been his secret marriage, five years
earlier, to the cripple Marie Lebyatkin. The scandal that ends
part I culminates in his denial of this marriage. Most of the cast
arrive, amid mounting speculation and excitement, in Mrs
Stavrogin's grand drawing-room, including three of the four
women with whom Stavrogin has had some kind of love-
passage: Lisa, Dasha and Marie. Marie solicits Mrs Stavrogin's
attention at the cathedral and is taken home in a spirit of
competitive philanthropy, Lisa staging a scene so as to be
allowed to accompany them. The energy here comes from the
ways in which the secret of Stavrogin's marriage to Marie –
which the reader may have guessed at, but has never been
told – is threatened with exposure. Since we are unsure what
the secret is, the suspense and the comedy alike are complicated.
The very fact of Marie's presence there, with her unaccountable
mixture of guilelessness and percipience, witnesses the impossible
liaison. Mrs Drozdov then hints at it with venom, and Lebyatkin
with clownish ineptitude. The crisis is postponed by the arrival
of Peter, closely followed by Stavrogin, who defuses the situation
with quiet skill and takes Marie home. Peter endorses Stavrogin's
lie with impudent chatter, Lisa laughs with a quality of erotic
attention-seeking and hysteria. Peter exposes his father, whom
Mrs Stavrogin then banishes. Shatov hits Stavrogin violently,

on his return, at which the latter controls himself with superhuman strength. Lisa faints.

The scene proceeds by a series of jolting, contradictory shocks. Dostoevsky the moralist fears and hates disorder; as an artist, however, he secretly revels in and exploits an energetic moral anarchy as few writers have done.

Where Stavrogin is concerned, we watch the apparent amoralist reacting with respect and chivalrous gentleness to the disturbed Marie; and with inhuman forebearance to Shatov's violent attack on him. In this he contrasts especially with Peter Verkhovensky, who was once spat at by Shatov and later murders him, partly out of spiteful revenge for this indignity, although nominally to protect the secret revolutionary cell Shatov has left and seems about to betray. Stavrogin, by contrast, knows how to swallow his own malice. When challenged to a duel by the irate Gaganov, he makes no attempt to avoid Gaganov's bullets, or to retaliate in kind to Gaganov's fury and hatred, which itself fills Gaganov with a more poisonous anger. Does such a mode of being testify to self-sacrifice or to further caprices of the will? Or both? We are left to decide for ourselves.

In the 'Night' section in part II, the ambiguities of Stavrogin's behaviour receive some focusing; not through any direct account of his mind, but through his colloquies with two characters who bear his influence and may mirror aspects of his thinking, Shatov and Kirilov. Both are Romantic solitaries, tormented by God or by godlessness, both equipped with firearms and with apocalyptic and *ersatz* private religions, although these are opposed. Both have flirted with the nihilists, though Shatov has since defected. They are linked together in other ways, having shared a spell in the USA, always for Dostoevsky a by-word for a 'progressive' hell – 'spiritualism, lynch law, six-shooters, hoboes' (1.4.4), 'a cess-pool' (II.1.7).

Stavrogin pays his night visits accompanied by an umbrella, in a book full of umbrellas. Mrs Stavrogin takes one with her *en route* between Dasha and Stepan Trofimovich; and the latter goes on his last pilgrimage with this comically mundane symbol of human vulnerability to outside event, of genteel dignity and of travel, in an intensely restless novel that starts in 'airiness' and ends in flight and death.

Just before these night journeyings, Stavrogin's mother

discovers him in a state of corpse-like immobility (II.1.4) that comes to seem a concrete metaphor for his state of mind. His round of calls begins with Kirilov, whom he needs to act as 'second' in his duel with Gaganov. Kirilov is a destitute structural engineer, unfussed by his poverty, an epileptic who is possessed, in part, of a good heart. He stops Lebyatkin beating his sister, and is touched by the late return of Shatov's wife to bear a child. He speaks in his philosophising, in a strange, 'Westernised' expatriate Russian, for a mystic's sense of universal harmony: 'A leaf's good. All's good' (II.1.5), which might link him with Myshkin's reverence for life, except that in Kirilov this is accompanied by a private theology of suicide-as-ultimate-freedom, which has proved fascinating to existentialists with their cult of extremity,[14] but reads as unhinged to ordinary mortals. Kirilov's death-wish mirrors Stavrogin's, and his final suicide may be a defiant imitation of Christ. To Peter Verkhovensky, more mundanely, its use is that Kirilov has agreed to sign any confession useful to (and exculpating) the revolutionaries, before carrying out the act.

Shatov, whom Stavrogin now visits, to warn of the danger to his life from the nihilists whose cause he has abandoned, is another monomaniac, the son of a serf, proud, clumsy and deserted by his beloved wife. His Slavophil views are superficially much closer to Dostoevsky's own, but with a satirical exaggeration that deprives us of much security. His author endorses his rejection of the progressive cause, as he does the moment when, after a frenzied attack on Stavrogin, he tells the latter to find God through work. Both his attack and his pleas – echoing Sonya to Raskolnikov – stem from his intuition that Stavrogin has lost the distinction between good and evil. Like Stepan Verkhovensky at the end, Kirilov speaks for forgiveness. He also identifies socialism and atheism, and attacks the desiccations of 'reason' and the coming despotism of 'half-science', pleading instead for a religious vision of man possessed by the 'spirit of life'. Dostoevsky hands him over to caricature, however, when he allows him, foaming at the mouth, to reduce God – in whom he does not 'yet' believe – to an attribute of nationality.

Both Kirilov and Shatov attest how much Stavrogin has meant to them in their lives. So, next, does Lebyatkin, Stavrogin's 'Falstaff' in his revels. Lebyatkin's worship of

Stavrogin is more purely comic, as are his own private attempts at evolving a metaphysic – culminating in his announced intention of bequeathing his skin to be made into a drum for the American national anthem to be daily beaten out on. Dostoevsky's 'doubles' are often most successful when at least touched by the comic in some form. The *political* posturings of *The Devils* betray their own sinister airiness, but the *metaphysical* posturings of Kirilov and Shatov prove vulnerable to humourless reading. Their heartless and passionate questioning of the conditions of life has appealed to contemporary taste, which has not always equally appreciated the 'Homeric laughter' that might accompany such questioning.

It is noteworthy here that Stavrogin, who influences Shatov and Kirilov, the most forward-looking as well as the most Romantic of Dostoevsky's heroes of the will, seems more than anything else to fear *being laughed at*. In the banned chapter Bishop Tikhon intuits his fear of being ridiculed beyond all else; and Lisa, after their failed night of love together late in the book, also realises that his 'secret sin' might well be something that makes him ridiculous. 'I shall make a laughing-stock of you' (III.2.1).

Twice during his round of night-visits, Fedka, the escaped convict, importunes him, armed with a knife, and ready to kill on Stavrogin's behalf, for money. 'Go on killing, go on stealing – go on!' (II.2.4), Stavrogin encourages him, and gives him the money that Fedka will later interpret as a bribe to rid him of the Lebyatkins, brother and sister. Stavrogin speaks of Fedka as 'one little devil' (II.3.4).

In a book full of such minor demons, the role of major devil is played by Peter Verkhovensky. Stavrogin and Peter are, respectively, the formed and the unformed results of Stepan Verkhovensky's attention. While Stavrogin was tutored by him, Peter, on the other hand, was, as he complains, sent off as a baby by parcel-post and then robbed of his inheritance. He shares his father's restless chatter, but where his father's persiflage is, in intention, innocent and aimless, his own ceaseless babble is purposeful and malevolent. Indeed the narrator speculates that his tongue, like the Devil's, must be unusually long, thin, red and sharp-tipped (I.5.5).

He has the gift of finding the weak spots of others and playing on them – vanity and social ambition in the case of the women; fear, or whatever comes to hand, in the case of the nihilists. Mrs Stavrogin at once prepares for long and ecstatic talks with him. The Governor's wife, Julia von Lembke, feels that he is enslaved to her without noticing that he has in fact wound her around his little finger. Throughout the book he is described as rushing, hurrying, rattling, wriggling, and seen as a demon clown, both ignoble and possessed.

It is Kirilov who sees that there comes a point where Peter ceases to be a clown and starts to be transformed into a madman. For the reader, this occurs during 'Ivan the Crown-Prince', after Virginsky's birthday party, at which he has carefully engineered the public shaming and exclusion of Shatov. 'You're my sun, I'm your worm' (II.8), he tells Stavrogin, whose power and beauty he is ready to worship, and to use for the purposes of the Revolution. Stavrogin's flinging him to the ground does not halt his rodomontade about the coming enslavement of the masses through Shigalyov's doctrine of terror and institutionalised depravity. 'We shall proclaim destruction . . . because the idea is so fascinating.'

For what does he stand? Soviet critics have (understandably) seen in him a proto-fascist, while others have seen in his ravings a prediction of Stalinism. But the book makes as much sense as a modern morality play as it does as a sequence of political prophecies. Here Peter plays Mephistopheles to Stavrogin's Faust, in a world in which Envy, Hatred, Greed and Vanity, together with other vices, threaten to take over in a general feast of misrule. In this world Peter is architect of darkness and disorder, and politics a set of ideological excuses for bad behaviour, shamelessness and solipsism.

Dostoevsky based Peter's character on Nechaev, who had had Ivanov murdered. But, so far from accurately representing nineteenth-century terrorist politics, Dostoevsky has everything every way. The organisation Peter represents is at once huge and puny, laughably powerless and vastly threatening, consisting of only one cell of five members in 'our town' – although there are, bewilderingly, eight persons involved – and of many such cells elsewhere. In this it reflects the 'vast anti-Government society of thirteen members' with which Stepan Verkhovensky may once have been involved, dangerous yet laughably innocuous at the same time, as well as Dostoevsky's own

youthful involvement with the Petrashevtsy. Peter's crew of
fools are 'paper men' to Shatov, 'shriekers' to Stepan, and
'trash' to Peter himself; and yet their machinations leave the
stage littered with corpses and insanity at the end.

Just as Dostoevsky equivocates about the size of the threat
the terrorists represent, so he jests about its ideological
complexion. Liputin is typical. He is a vain, restless
scandalmonger and Peter's furtive henchman until at the end
he tries to flee. He is throughout characterised as miserly and
acquisitive and, 'above all, a capitalist and a money-lender'
(III.4.4). Dostoevsky thus gives the group the traditional vices
both of the new (to Russia) capitalist class (greed) and of the
Left (envy), and then adds some extra. The new writers who
burst in in part I give a foretaste of things to come: treacherous,
spiteful and vain *on principle*, they discuss reforms to the
alphabet, the constitution, Poland, and also – and enviously –
Krayevsky's splendid house, 'for which no one seemed able to
forgive Mr Krayevsky' (I.1.6). These New Men are typified by
wounded pride and bitterness (II.7.1), vanity (II.8), envy and
hatred (I.5.4). 'Everywhere we see vanity reaching enormous
proportions, enormous bestial appetites' (II.8).

This spectacular growth of vanity, indeed, affects governors
and governed, reactionary and revolutionary, alike. It is
especially on show in the scandalous party-scenes, which have
so little of the reassuring quality they present in Dickens, that
other delighted chronicler of the mess and jumble of human
conviviality. Here, once more, they are mostly opportunities for
the exchange of wounds and the indecent exposure of private
hurts. Peter (with some justice) mocks Julia's desire to 'unite
society' through parties (III.2.2): for him any such future
unification, as for Shigalyov, will occur only by virtue of the
total enslavement of the Many to the Few. The nihilists who
preach the New Millennium at Virginsky's birthday party
are powered by hatred, spite and a talent for farcical
inconsequentiality. Shigalyov, the ominous and dejected
philosopher, plans to read his *magnum opus* over ten evenings in
public. Peter cuts his nails during the meeting, which is also
not a meeting, and then engineers the freezing-out of Shatov, in
a chilling sequence that prefigures his murder. The others airily
discuss the origin of thunder, and the origin of the family, in a

mood of encyclopaedic and conceited rationalism that recalls a yet more frenzied version of Jonathan Swift's Academy of Lagado in *Gulliver's Travels*.

Part II sees other premonitory stirrings: the appearance of buffoons and scoffers and madcaps in a mood halfway between a students' rag and full Saturnalia: pranks, cavalcades, small adventures of the imagination and the will ensue. One escapade involves the publicising of an unusual wedding-night, another the insertion of obscene photographs into the gospels that Sophia Ulitin is selling; anarchic music is composed, jewels belonging to an icon are stolen and a live mouse inserted in the case. The visit to sight-see at a holy fool is delayed by the sight-seeing of a corpse. A second lieutenant is reported who bites his officer's shoulder and has a mad private religion, a cult of the New nationalism. Through all this, Peter's machinations redouble. Fire and disease are the concrete metaphors Dostoevsky employs to figure the epidemic growth of disorder: both are actual, both point to the spreading, depersonalising qualities of the approaching chaos. 'The fire's in the minds of the people', says von Lembke when, despite having gone mad, he speaks true (III.2.4).

Part II ends with the raid on Stepan's apartments, by which he is more alarmed than flattered, and by his comical confrontation with the von Lembkes, dominating self-deluded wife and increasingly impotent, shrill Governor–husband. Lisa challenges Stavrogin, once more, about his relations with the Lebyatkins, and, just as part I ended (roughly) with his denial of the truth, this ends with his equally arbitrary public avowal of it, to the shock of the assembled company, especially his mother.

Part III is prefaced by an extraordinary list of the social 'scum' now rising to the surface and dominating events – a catalogue of Dostoevsky's *bêtes noires*, from feminists and seminarians to 'wretched little Jews': the atmosphere now seething with palpable impatience, malice and evil. We note a curious echo between Lyamshin and the Russified German bureaucrat von Lembke. Lyamshin, a nihilist, is much in demand for his imitations – he can mimic a pig, a thunderstorm, a confinement with the first cry of a baby, Stepan Verkhovensky as a liberal-of-the-1840s, 'various kinds of Jew'. Von Lembke, the footling Governor, has his own party-tricks. As a student he was famous for being untidy in a specially witty way, for playing overtures on his nose and for making obscene *tableaux vivants* in the dormitory. As an adult he consoles himself for loss of a girl by making an animated cardboard theatre, and consoles himself for his failure as a novelist by making a 'most successful' model of a railway train – 'the passengers with their children and dogs, carrying trunks and bags, came out on the platform and got into the carriages' (II.4.3). He has a comic double, another 'unlucky' German, called Blum, who has the same name and patronymic as himself and is much hated by von Lembke's conceited wife Julia. It is Blum who mistakenly orders the raiding of Verkhovensky *père* instead of Verkhovensky *fils*. The little scene in which, at the height of the crisis, he trips on his rug and then shouts at the rug, 'Have it changed!' is pure Charlie Chaplin in the *Great Dictator*. Yet 'Have it changed!', of reality, or of the world, is in a sense what most of the characters, fantasists to a man, are airily saying. Von Lembke is not the only character constructing novel 'toy' universes.

His relations with his wife form one in a chain of cruel and humiliating relationships: Stepan Trofimovich and Mrs Stavrogin; Lisa Tushin and her fiancée Drozdov, whom she publicly humiliates; Stavrogin and Peter, who seems to enjoy the other's contempt for him; Marie Shatov and her husband, whom she returns to and abuses. Moreover, the posturing hysteria and airy futility of the governing class here mirror the militant hysteria and fatuity of the nihilists. And a mixture of vanity and foolishness causes the governing classes to flirt with the 'new ideas'. Stepan is tormented by Chernyshevsky's *What is to be Done?* with its apparent corruption of his generation's idealism. Mrs Stavrogin charges him with having kept such new ideas from her and with 'hindering progress', and attacks his aestheticism. Julia von Lembke farcically believes in a *rapprochement* between new and old values. Karmazinov, mad with vanity, toadies uncertainly to the new. Even von Lembke owns 'pamphlets' which he fears may compromise him. And Lisa plans to start a journal 'for the common cause'. One anonymous councillor might be taken as typifying this general collusion when he comically assures an assembled company that he has mysteriously fallen under the influence of the *Internationale* (III.1.1).

At the start of part III, disorder and farce are still firmly yoked. Karmazinov agrees to give a reading *en travestie* as a governess of our province. Julia is fascinated by the elaborate toasts she is composing. The band opens proceedings with a satirical pomp. Lebyatkin appears drunk on stage and provokes laughter with his 'free' verse. Karmazinov is barracked for reading an absurdly self-indulgent 'farewell' to his audience, in a poisonous satire of Turgenev's style. The audience then give Stepan Verkhovensky worse treatment as he rises to denounce the new values. 'Mankind can live without science, without bread, but without beauty it cannot carry on', echoing here Dostoevsky's own dearest views, views which in *The Idiot* partly attach to Myshkin.

By the evening, things have deteriorated further. An idiotic literary quadrille is performed, during which Lyamshin walks upside-down: but by this stage upside-downness dominates everything. The suburb across the river is set alight, von Lembke goes mad and orders his own wife's arrest, and the first of the murders are committed, a joyous destructiveness pervading the scene. Fits of screaming mark the *dénouement*. Stepan Verkhovensky had screamed shrilly when raided, and von Lembke screams 'absurdly' and shrilly at the insurrection he thinks is occurring. Now Lebyatkin has his throat cut, Marie is knifed, their maid has her skull smashed in. Fedka, who perpetrated this, is killed by his accomplice Fomka. Lisa is lynched by the mob outside the Lebyatkins after the failure of her night of love with Stavrogin. Shatov, who has been newly humanised for the reader, and filled with joy by the return of his wife to bear Stavrogin's child, in a marvellous, moving small scene, is shot by Peter Verkhovensky in the park. The full horror of this scene, at which both Lyamshin and Virginsky start to scream, is only exceeded by Kirilov's suicide. In this terrifying finale, Peter plays cat-and-mouse with the now insane Kirilov, the latter biting Peter's finger in a macabre and spectacularly horrible sequence, just before he shoots his own head off after agreeing to 'confess' to Shatov's murder. Marie Shatov and her baby die. Peter maligns Julia as a pander, and threatens the conspirators, by now half insane themselves with terror both at what they have done and at what may be to come.

The ending sees two kinds of travel, in a book abounding in journeys. Peter sneaks off by train, first-class, with his travelling-rug, pampered and specious and dangerous to the end. His rootlessness, for Dostoevsky, is intimately connected with his diabolism, and both can be detected in his phrase – typical of the modish 1860s, in which shibboleths were so strongly attacked – 'without prejudices'. He assures Lisa that Drozdov will take her back as he is a man 'without prejudices' (III.3.3). The conspirators are assured not to worry about Kirilov taking the rap since 'he has no prejudices' (III.4.1); and Peter whips the conspirators further into line with the adage that 'no prejudices will stop each of us doing his duty' (III.4.3). The airy fantasy of being without prejudices, of being cultureless, recalls both Chernyshevsky's tiresomely unshockable 'rational' heroes and Bazarov's refusal to take anything on trust in Turgenev's *Fathers and Sons*. The phrase is in any case mocked by Peter himself when he provokes the nihilists at Virginsky's birthday party simply by publicly cutting his nails. And the phrase links the end of the book to its beginning, where the odious new writers wished to abolish 'inheritance, the family, children and the priesthood' (I.1.6), in one of Dostoevsky's joke lists: how do you 'abolish' children? In Lisa's case, her fiancée Drozdov's generosity about her loss of virginity (exactly one such prejudice) does not stop her from being lynched; in Kirilov's it is exactly his want of 'prejudice' about suicide and perjury that makes us conclude that he is insane; while in the nihilists' their instinct for personal survival is happily deeper than Peter pretends to suppose.

Perhaps Peter really is 'without prejudices'. It may be this that makes him finally so unimaginable, in his inner being, to the reader. In this he contrasts with Stavrogin, whose lack of moral bearings causes him to hang himself with a carefully soaped rope. In his confession to Tikhon, he revealed himself as without the 'prejudices' of good and evil. Both, here, contrast with Stepan Verkhovensky's picaresque 'last pilgrimage', away from free-thinking, and towards old dogma. Equipped only with epigrams and his umbrella, he is given further encounters with pain, grief, the Gospels, and the rooted Russian 'Folk' whom he had until then neglected; and his dying within reach of the village of Spasov (i.e. village of the Saviour), but not within sight of it, suggests such hope of regeneration as the book permits. He is made privy to the biblical quotations that, for Dostoevsky, help decode some of the action – God's rejection

of the lukewarm in Revelation, which seems to bespeak
Stavrogin's damnation through his indifference more than his
depravity (III.7.2) – for Dostoevsky a *true* sinner would always
be closer to redemption than a mediocre one; and the quotation
from St Luke's Gospel about the Gadarene swine which provides
the novel with its very title and its epigraph, in which Jesus
exorcises one sufferer's evil spirits by causing them to enter into
and madden a pig-herd into mass suicide. The novel has
chronicled 'all the sores, all the poisonous exhalations . . .
impurities, all the big and little devils' (III.7.2) that have
tormented his beloved Russia.

And yet the energy of the book, comic once more here after
the horrors which precede it, belies such tidiness. Stepan
himself, apostate to the last, is set not merely to preach the
Gospels, but to improve on their 'understandable' errors(!),
explaining to the Gospel woman how happiness doesn't pay
him, since he starts at once forgiving all his enemies. He also
fantasises, lies, manipulates, and preaches love and forgiveness
and humility, and is fulminated at by a furious and heart-
broken Mrs Stavrogin as 'you futile man, you futile, disgraceful,
cowardly, always, always futile man' (III.7.3). In a book in
which all the 'strong' types are of the Devil's party, however, he
is beloved to the end by his author, for his gentle, unresentful
heart.

The existentialists hailed Dostoevsky as a forefather because
he seemed the first to preach the 'Absurd' – the affront that the
pointless contingency of life offers to the startled ego. Kirilov's
'A leaf's good; all's good' is a long way from that particular
vision, and a long way, too, from what Dostoevsky enacts in his
fiction, with its relative neglect of the natural world. And yet, in
his delighted celebration of the details, funny, horrible, absurd –
in an ordinary, non-metaphysical sense – of Verkhovensky's life
and of his dying, he goes a long way beyond such metaphysical
self-pity.

6

The Brothers Karamazov (1880)

Dostoevsky's last novel is also his greatest, and among the greatest of all novels. Its moral passion has a sublime grandeur, its story a sensational, stark beauty. A passionate simplicity marks its delineation of character, while its themes – religious faith and doubt, love and rebellion, disintegration and renewal, and, above all, the terrible mysteries of good and evil – are intricately 'worked'. It is a novel about the murder of a father by his own child (parricide), and a massive false trail leads the reader to believe, against his will, that Mitya must have perpetrated this act. We read, therefore, for suspense at the level of story, as well as for metaphysical suspense at the level of idea-play. The centre of this idea-play (atheism) and the subject of the story (parricide), moreover, echo each other: each concerns the overthrow of the father, earthly or heavenly, the rejection of authority, human and divine. In Siberia Dostoevsky had been much struck by Ilyinsky, a convict falsely convicted for parricide. His own father's death may have left him with an unquiet conscience: his father's estate contained the village of Chermashnya, which figures on the Karamazov estate and is associated by both Ivan and Mitya with their guilt.[15]

The story builds the clarity of a folk-tale into a complex picture, as Dostoevsky intended, of contemporary educated Russia. There are three brothers, one sensual (Mitya), one clever (Ivan), and the youngest and best-beloved, who is most good (Alyosha). Much of the action moves in threes: besides the three brothers, there are three girls (Katerina, Lise, Grushenka), each of whom is courted by or attracted to, two Karamazov men; three chapters of confession that Mitya makes to Alyosha, and a further three made by Ivan to Alyosha; three ordeals Mitya suffers when arrested; three interviews between Ivan and the true murderer, his half-brother, the illegitimate

Smerdyakov. Threes haunt the book, too, in the figure of 3000 rubles, the sum Katerina gives Mitya to mail to her, but which he partly squanders and then desperately tries to raise; the sum Karamazov keeps to bribe Grushenka to come to him; the extra sum he wishes to get from the peasant Lyagavy for a wood; the sum Mitya offers Grushenka's Polish seducer, to bribe him to leave her; the sum Mitya is thought to have stolen from his father when he murdered him. Even the Petersburg lawyer's fee for defending Mitya is 3000 rubles.

The first of the twelve constituent books gives us family history, and the second the preliminary scandal at the monastery where Alyosha attends the good and dying Zossima. The action, as usual, moves in concentrated bursts of time – from the scandal to the murder is four days; Mitya's trial and young Ilyusha's death in the last book constitute another compressed band of time.

The novel is set in the town of Skotoprigonyevsk – meaning 'the beast-pen' – where Fyodor Pavlovich Karamazov has fathered a number of sons. He is a dissolute small landowner, an ill-natured and licentious clown, preposterous and muddle-headed in, we are told, the Russian style. He marries Adelaida Miusov, beautiful, wealthy and a girl of character, and cheats her out of her 25,000-ruble inheritance. She had eloped with him from caprice, and, following the marriage's failure, runs away with a graduate of a religious seminary, abandoning her three-year-old child, Mitya. Karamazov neglects the child, turning his home into a bawdy-house, holding orgies of drinking and general misbehaviour. Despite his debauchery and general neglect of Mitya, Dostoevsky takes care to warn us early on that, like all wrongdoers – 'like we, ourselves' – he was more naïve and artless than we generally assume (1.1). Here Dostoevsky warns us against facile judgements: he seeks not merely our belief, as readers, but also our direct involvement.

Karamazov's second marriage is to the sixteen-year-old beauty Sophia Ivanovna, an orphan who has attempted suicide to evade her tormenting and tyrannical 'protectress'. His behaviour now deteriorates. He invites whores home for orgies while his wife is in the house. She understandably develops a nervous disease, and dies after eight years of maltreatment, leaving two sons, Ivan and Alyosha, to suffer a similar neglect to that already undergone by Mitya. All three are brought up by servants and distant relatives. At the point where the plot begins, the family meet up again, and more or less as complete strangers, whose discovery of one another forms a major strand in the story.

One further episode in Karamazov's life is chronicled. Coming home one evening in a company of 'gay young blades', he encounters a solitary half-wit, 'stinking Lizaveta' (III.2) and, in response to a bet, rapes her, while the mourning-band for his first wife is still on his hat. Since the cook, Smerdyakov, who kills Karamazov, is the child of this perverse union, the novel has been read as one of moral come-uppance: his mother dies in childbirth, in wretchedness and misery, while the son later takes revenge for the father's multiple betrayals. But this grossly simplifies the tale, which scarcely advocates vengeance, and which does not emphasise this world as a place in which merit is necessarily rewarded or vice punished. No consoling victory in the perpetual battle between good and evil is promised, either in the individual heart or at large: only, at best, a renewal of the necessary struggle.

Mitya, the eldest, was taken in by the servant Grigory, then by his cousin Miusov, who early recounts Karamazov's seeming puzzlement that he even had a son. Miusov, too, then forgets about him and, after two further 'adoptions', a riotous army career complete with duel and demotion to the ranks, Mitya becomes involved in a lengthy struggle with his father over his inheritance from his wealthy mother. The father fobs off the son with occasional handouts, which the son regards as interest on his birthright, while the wilier father accounts them as discharging his debt.

The scandalous scene that opens the tale is set in the local monastery, where Alyosha is the favourite of the elder Zossima, the novel's dying saint and spokesman for the good life, in the truest sense. Karamazov has jokingly proposed this venue as an apt one for him and Mitya to make up their differences. What ensues is among the most painful and comical of Dostoevsky's scenes of scandal, containing a notable prophetic moment. Karamazov has by this stage degenerated both in appearance and in inner life, to an arrogant, bloated and inconsequential clown, with a long, cruel mouth, full lips and black, decaying stumps of teeth, and the general *mien* of a decadent Roman.

Ivan, Karamazov and Miusov, a foolish, rich 1840s liberal

with his inadequate 'culture', arrive first. Karamazov is full of sniggering innuendo. He has already been established for us as a man who plays his best respects to religion and the Ideal through blasphemous parody – when his first wife died he had shouted the opening of the *Nunc dimittis*: 'Lord, now lettest Thou Thy servant depart in peace' (i.1). He now develops a running joke about monasteries, with concubines and secret passages to 'the ladies'.

On arrival he mimics Miusov's 'society' bow to the monks, and this prepares us for the monkey-like role he plays throughout: the aping of the 'higher' by the 'lower' the negative but comic tribute paid by vice to virtue. Dostoevsky's surely intends the comedy just as much as he intends us to see Karamazov's antics as perverse and destructive. In pretending homage to the good Zossima, 'Holy elder', 'your reverence', 'blessed man' and 'most holy being' are some of the terms he invents, undermining honour through excess, to both our acute embarrassment and our delight. He renews this strategy when he unexpectedly kneels and asks how he can gain eternal life, and when, in mock-religious language, he blesses the womb that bore Zossima and especially the 'tits' that 'gave thee suck'.

He tells pointless, banal puns, tests the elder through a mock-artless question about a martyred saint purported to have kissed his own decapitated head, acts the saintly fool – the point about a *true* saintly fool being precisely that, unlike Karamazov, he would be unwitting. Karamazov's antics display his profound insincerity, and his lack of any real peace of conscience. 'A disgraceful comedy', Mitya exclaims when he belatedly arrives (ii.6), and Karamazov explains, with an insolent humility, that he has staged this comedy of disgrace in order to test Zossima – after also proposing that he makes a fool of himself in order to be better liked. Neither explanation exhausts his complex motives, and Zossima, dealing with the situation with a patient good cheer despite the fact that he is ill and dying, advises him to cease lying.

Zossima momentarily leaves the Karamazov contingent to attend to some patiently waiting peasant woman. One poor woman has lost all four of her children but cannot cease grieving for the last. This is an important, as well as a harrowing, scene, for both Ivan and Zossima are to preach on the death and suffering of children. 'If only I could see him', she exclaims, and is advised to allow time to heal her. A second awaits news of her son in Siberia and is told, accurately, that he is still alive. The scene introduces the themes of faith and of patient suffering. The suffering of children, in particular, stands in this novel as the *ne plus ultra* of evil and of incomprehensible human pain.

The scene is at once followed, in the dialectic that marks this novel, by 'A Lady of Little Faith'. Here the effusive, wildly funny and profoundly troubled Khokhlakova – mother of the crippled Lise – naïvely exposes her doubts. Zossima advises her to practice active love, in order to develop her faith, rather than wait, before improving herself, for her faith to be made perfect. In this novel, faith produces miracle: miracle should not be thought of as a bribe to induce faith. But what if the patient she is nursing, she reasonably asks, begins to torment her with his whims, rather than showering her with gratitude? 'In short, I can work only if I am paid. I demand payment at once' (II.4).

Perhaps related to the fact that she is a comic character, she has the honesty to express the deep human fear that her virtue may go unrewarded. She ignores the unpalatable fact that virtue which seeks a reward is no longer virtuous. Her fears were echoed, Zossima tells her, by a doctor who found that, the more he loved humanity in the abstract, the harder he found it to love individuals. Within twenty-four hours of intimate contact he had discovered that it was possible to hate even the best man – because of the way he blew his nose or sat too long at his dinner. And both Khokhlakova and the doctor are later to be echoed by Ivan, when he observes that 'a man's *face* banishes love' (v.4).

Similarly, Mitya's murderous hatred of his father is fuelled by sight of his 'pendulous Adam's apple, hooked nose' and lewdly expectant lips (VIII.4). It is profoundly observed that hatred, like love, feeds on *detail*, and Dostoevsky, like so many Russian novelists, is the apostle of details, details delighted in, obfuscated, or held up, like the fly on Nastasya's corpse, for our horror. Rakitin tells Alyosha that men have ruined themselves not merely for a woman's body, but for one *part* of her body: desire, too, feeds on detail. And so does love. When Ivan explains his passionate love of life, it is the 'sticky little leaves' of spring he is to recall. Detail rescues this huge novel from an excess of formal symmetry; while, at the same time, the perception that love and hate feed off detail, maps out, as it were, the moral space of the book, which is bounded on either side by love and by egoism, and which pictures the soul, more vividly than before, as embattled between these.

Ivan has watched proceedings in the monastery with a heartless curiosity and a detached indifference. Discussion now turns to a two-faced article that he has written, about ecclesiastical courts, and the relations between Church and State. Zossima sees swiftly and deeply into Ivan's bitter self-division. There is, in Ivan's article, a more formidable version of the mock-seriousness practised by his father. In private Ivan has been preaching that, with the collapse of religious dogma – belief in God and in immortality – all moral sanction will cease and 'everything would be permitted, even cannibalism' (II.5). Ivan's is the *intellectual* vision of the total shamelessness and total solipsism that his father has flirted with in practice, and which offers no barrier against the depths of evil in the human heart. The fierce love of life shared by all the Karamazovs bears an equivocal relation to the amoralism Ivan preaches. It at least invites a continuing connection with the world and with other people, to be set against the isolation into which Zossima sees humankind as increasingly falling. But love of life on its own offers no moral safeguards, either. It cannot, by itself, help Ivan's own isolation.

Mitya's late arrival brings both the metaphysical discussion and the human plot to a crisis. Ivan's secret beliefs are exposed. And so is the bitter hatred and rivalry between Mitya and his father, competing both for money and for the beautiful Grushenka. Mitya denounces his father as a dissolute rake and a contemptible clown, adding, 'Why does such a man live? . . . Can he be allowed to defile the earth by his existence?' (II.6), upon which Mitya is unmasked, in his turn, by his father as a potential parricide. It is at this point that Zossima prostrates himself before Mitya, even touching the ground with his forehead, acknowledging, as he later confesses to Alyosha, the great sufferings that he intuits may be in store for the young man. The mysterious and perhaps terrible meaning of this act is much discussed. Zossima tells Alyosha, on his own, that he will have to leave the monastery and marry, to 'know great sorrow and in that sorrow to be happy' (II.7).

The prattling, cynical, pruriently inquisitive and envious Rakitin now quizzes Alyosha about his virginity. Sensualists

such as his brother Mitya or his father, Rakitin tells him, will
forfeit everything in the world, not merely for a woman, but for
love of one part of her body; Alyosha, too, admits to experiencing
desire, and Rakitin introduces the story of Mitya and the rich
Katerina, whom Mitya has capriciously humiliated, in return
for money he whimsically decided to give to save her father's
reputation. Katerina fell in love with Mitya – or, masochistically,
with his treatment of her; Ivan, too, is in love with Katerina. It
will later appear important that, if anything were to happen to
Karamazov, Grushenka might then accept Mitya, thus releasing
Katerina for him. Ivan, too, has a vested interest in his father's
demise.

Meanwhile, at the Father Superior's dinner, Karamazov
stages a further scandal, provoking Miusov, teasing the fat old
liar Maximov – in whom he perhaps recognises his own
double – pretending to mistake him for a voluptuary recently
murdered in a brothel. He tries to bury his recent shame in yet
further shamelessness, denouncing as parasites the monks whom
he has recently supported with a gift and who are entertaining
him lavishly. Book II ends with disgrace, and a disorderly exit.

*   *   *

The opening section of the novel is richly comical and full of
foreboding. It presents the major themes of the book. Here
might also be identified the strategy of the argument, which is a
paradoxical one. Dostoevsky now takes what could be called his
'strategy of the obverse' to its extremest point. That is to say,
he defends his best beliefs, his own pieties, at their weakest
point, and by testing them to near breaking-point. He defends
the institution of the family, much under attack by nihilists, in
a cautionary tale about a broken family that is a laughable,
grotesque parody of happy family life. Karamazov has neglected
both wives and children. His sons scarcely know one another.
The father is a monster of clownish greed and low cunning,
insolence, lust and cruelty. Son is pitted against father, and
brother against brother, in erotic and monetary intrigue.
Dostoevsky defends the idea of limited free will – for him, an
essentially religious idea – by showing men driven by passion,
distorted by greed. He defends the idea of reason within a
canvas of frenetic irrationality. He defends the idea of faith by

displaying it under the most devastating attack. Above all, he defends the 'Higher', the 'Ideal', the idea of moral regeneration itself, associated throughout with Schiller, who is cited by Karamazov (II.6, 8), Mitya (III.3) and Ivan (IV.5), through the most radical subversion of it so far.

The Devil has many guises in the novel. There are minor devils in the cynical Rakitin, and in the murderous Smerdyakov, who used as a child to hang cats and then bury them with sacrilegious ceremony; and as an adult teaches the local children to torture starving dogs by feeding them bread containing a bent pin. Ferapont sees devils everywhere. Ivan has a waking nightmare of being visited by the Devil in person, in book XI, at the moment when his guilt first becomes apparent to him and just before he is maddened by it. Above all, Ivan launches his famous attack on the Ideal, through his prose-poem of the Grand Inquisitor in book V, after condemning a universe in which children are tortured and horribly murdered for casual 'fun' or active sadism or both. The Grand Inquisitor may be taken as an avatar of Satan, too, in the original sense of the name: 'Satan' means 'adversary'. He is the dark double of Jesus Christ, and the underside of that 'great idealist'. The book's vision of evil, altogether, is as compelling as its vision of faith and goodness. Ivan's Devil in book XI may be said to describe the moral structure of the novel, as well as his own supposed function in the universe, when he tells Ivan, in marvellous and unforgettable language, that it is his (the Devil's) role to provide an 'indispensable minus sign' and 'to try the Hosannahs of God in the crucible of doubt'.

Similarly the novel tests its own 'Hosannahs' – its own positives and best beliefs – in the crucible of its own scepticism. And many critics have reacted to it as did T. S. Eliot with Tennyson's *In Memoriam*: finding it religious because of the intense and searing quality of its own doubt, quite as much as because of the quality of its faith.[16]

*   *   *

The pole of faith is defended and represented by the good Zossima, whose swift decomposition after his death in book IV precipitates a second scandal: it was superstitiously believed that the bodies of saints did not rapidly putrefy. Zossima marks

a departure for Dostoevsky. In the past his powerful speakers –
such as the Underground Man – were often amoral; while his
good characters – such as Sonya and Myshkin – were
inconclusive in speech. Zossima is both a good and an
authoritative teacher and, in this as in other things, opposed to
Karamazov, as good and bad father-figures respectively.
Karamazov is a sentimental old hypocrite with a needless love
of dissembling, a wicked garrulity, a boastful self-abasement
and a tendency to lust, a vice associated in this novel with the
cruelty of insects. A profaner of things holy, he had desecrated
his second wife's icon by spitting at it and defying 'God' to
punish him (III.8). He attacks the monks in book II and demands
that Alyosha leave the monastery.

Zossima, too, instructs Alyosha to leave, but after a different
style. He is, by contrast, a chaste talker, who waits his occasion
and makes his speech 'tell'. He is full of wise counsel, both for
those who seek it from him, and – as Dostoevsky clearly
intended – for the reader. He is the spokesman for two related
kinds of good advice – about morality and about happiness.
Thus, though he is presented as a soul-doctor, an expert on the
human soul who knows at a glance his visitors' troubles, his
advice always noticeably cheers up its recipients and makes
them happy. He is given Dostoevsky's own fears – of a scientific-
rationalist future from which faith has disappeared, void of any
spiritual vision; of the growth of crimes which no transcendent
faith remains to check; of the identification of crime with mere
environmentally determined 'social protest', enfeebling to the
sense of free will. He fears, too, the new human isolation that
he sees as the fruit of a growing individualism. For him, hell is
the inability to love, an impotence which such an isolating
individualism both grows out of and feeds. And love itself is the
cure of both. Karamazov's, of course, is one such painful
isolation, his evenings cheered up mainly by the rats he likes to
watch at play; while Zossima's secluded life deep in the woods
is, by contrast, spiritual and fruitful to his many visitors. Some
of his prophecy now looks quaint – for example, the peasantry
are to cure the intelligentsia by reconverting it to Orthodoxy;
much seems perennially fresh.

For Zossima, guilt unites all humanity and must be embraced
with joy.[17] He again and again preaches that each man must be
accountable for all, must make himself responsible for his

neighbour's sins. In this way sin, he argues, can be countered with love, and not by the external punishment of the State. Echoing Myshkin, he calls a loving humility a 'terrible force'. The joy accompanying his belief is central. Although ill and shortly to die, he is presented himself as full of joy, and is grateful to Alyosha when the latter tells him he looks cheerful. 'You couldn't have said anything that would have made me so happy. For men are made for happiness. . . . All the righteous, all the saints, all the martyrs, were happy people' (II.4). When Alyosha at his lowest point is visited and consoled by a revelatory dream of the dead Zossima – each of the brothers has an apt and 'significant' dream – it is notably a joyous dream of Cana in Galilee, where Christ himself 'makes merry with us, turns water into wine, so as not to cut short the gladness of the guests' (VII.4). Indeed, those few souls in Dostoevsky who seem wholly beyond the reach of their author's sympathy – Luzhin, Rakitin, Smerdyakov – are always joyless as much as bad.

Zossima's vision of a happy spirituality – strictly speaking a heterodox one (see, for example, Berdyaev, 1957, pp. 205ff.; and Sutherland, 1977, pp. 132–6) – is offensive to more ascetic souls, such as the monk from Obdorsk with his needling scepticism, or Ferapont, whose fear of the flesh has denatured him. These latter triumph in the untimely decomposition of Zossima's body in book VII, and use it for political ends, exemplifying again the envy born by lesser men against the Ideal. What a man *is* here affects his vision, and *vice versa*, so that the mediocre rationalist Miusov, too, sees not Zossima's holiness, but a 'spiteful, petty, supercilious person' who discomforts him (II.2).

While Zossima's death in book VII raises questions of faith, Karamazov's in book VIII raises questions at the level of the story. Who killed him? Why? And will Mitya be convicted for it? This plot and the idea-play begin to intersect when it becomes slowly apparent that, although Smerdyakov actually committed the murder, responsibility for it has to be claimed and shared by Alyosha, Mitya and Ivan alike, in different ways and for different reasons.

Dostoevsky originally conceived of Alyosha as the novel's hero, and gives him pride of place at the beginning and the last word in the epilogue. Yet Mitya and Ivan clearly grew in interest for him, too, until the book had three, joint heroes. Each lives by a different set of beliefs, and therefore sees a different universe, and lives accordingly. The story drives each of them through ordeal and suffering.

Alyosha is universally loved. Ivan tells him how much he loves his face. Mitya, in the deepest trouble, tells Alyosha that he loves him best of all, that his heart aches for him. Even his father, who is predisposed towards Ivan, comes to love Alyosha for seeing but not condemning or even outwardly judging him. The young nihilist Kolya dreams of Alyosha and loves him 'terribly' before meeting him. The 'fallen' Grushenka longs to meet him and regards him as her conscience. He is very handsome, a physical beauty signalling spiritual worth, just as Smerdyakov's ugliness is the sign of his spiritual sickness. In a not-untypical carelessness, he is either nineteen years old (1.5) or twenty (1.4). He is loved for many qualities. He never nurses grievances or resents the generosity of others. He is quixotic about money. He observes intently even the most terrible things – in which the book abounds – in silent suffering, seeing all, grieving inwardly. His very existence heartens others. Ivan tells him that it is enough for him that Alyosha exists, so that Ivan will not lose his desire for life.

In an unwritten sequel, Dostoevsky intended Alyosha to be tempted, to fall and to be redeemed – another variant on the life of a 'Great Sinner'. It is a mark of his moral realism that he resists the temptation to make Alyosha simply saintly. He shares the Karamazov sensuality – sharing with Zossima a love of 'sweet things', such as cherry jam, and is built, as Zossima sees, for marriage. Doubts about God's existence touch him as well as Ivan (v.1), and, influenced and disturbed by Ivan, he once repeats the latter's rejection of God's world (vii.2). His 'deep, ardent inner ecstasy' (1.5) is, at the start, partly adolescent high spirits, and he only weathers into maturity through being inwardly embattled. The scandal of Zossima's putrefaction affects him with inner anguish, rather than the jealous glee felt by others. Rakitin seizes on this moment of doubt and tempts him, against his vows, first to sausage, then to vodka, and finally to visit Grushenka, who had long wished to meet, and perhaps seduce, him. Rakitin wants twenty-five rubles for this introduction. Grushenka's reaction to the news of Zossima's death, which she hears about while seated on Alyosha's knee, comes with the force of a spiritual sign to them both (vii.3). She starts up in devotion and dismay, saving him from what, in an earlier talk (iii.4), he had described as a ladder of licentiousness, which resembles the spiritual ladder, but in reverse movement. Her faith makes friends of them instead, and she speaks of Alyosha as her conscience.

Grushenka's action might be taken as exactly such a tiny token of grace as properly proceeds from active faith – rather than, as Khokhlakova hungered to see, miracle *causing* faith. A similar 'sign' occurred on Alyosha's earlier requesting to see his mother's grave. Karamazov no longer even recalls where she is buried; and yet Alyosha's piety moves him to donate 1000 rubles to the monastery. Throughout the book, many characters are similarly impressionable. Karamazov absurdly claimed to have had his faith undermined – or what was left of it – by Miusov's story of the decapitated saint kissing his own head. Both Mitya and Smerdyakov are to be shown as genuinely disturbed by Ivan's message that 'all is permitted', and Smerdyakov murders, in part, to act out this adage. A digression in 'Devout Peasant Women' (ii.3) on the mechanics of faith showed how self-validating a strong sense of expectation could be, just as another aside (i.5) about the institution of confession showed it to be double-edged, leading either to humility and self-mastery, or, on the contrary, to the 'most satanic pride' (i.5). The self-assertive will loves to parody self-effacement, throughout Dostoevsky. But the book, with all its 'modern' sense of freedom, and of a world without guarantees, asserts both an ascending and a descending dialectic of faith and doubt. And, because it shows its characters as suggestible, shows them also as responsible for the effect their beliefs, or lack of them, have on others. The question of 'what you live by' tests and measures all the characters.

What Alyosha tries to live by is the practical love commanded by Zossima. He is arbiter, judge, kind witness, necessary observer. He listens to people and enables them to reveal themselves truthfully to him (and to the reader) and acts as messenger, passively open to the requirements of others. He thus advances both our knowledge of other characters, such as his brothers, who confess to him in books iii and v, and also acts as a Hermes Psychopompos, or angelic errand-boy, a leader of souls who advances the plot. Mitya requires him to visit Katerina, and bid her farewell, and to visit Karamazov and try to extract 3000 rubles from him, to discharge his debt to her. Lise Khokhlakov proposes to him and then later rejects him, charging him with being so compliant that he would, if married, carry notes from her to the next man she fell in love with. In his patience with Lise's perversities he meets a severe test.

He meets another on errand from Katerina to Snegirov, whom Mitya has wantonly assaulted and whom Katerina wishes, from impure motives of her own (to humble Mitya and advertise her own generosity), to help financially. Alyosha suffers the attack of Snegirov's son Ilyusha, dying of TB and maddened by Mitya's public humiliation of his father. Ilyusha bites Alyosha's finger to the bone, and his father also at first rejects the proffered financial help he desperately needs. By patiently absorbing the pain both father and son pass on to him, Alyosha helps them both. Snegirov is eventually able to swallow his hurt pride and accept the much-needed cash; and Alyosha is to befriend and console the dying Ilyusha, just as he does Ilyusha's school-fellows. The latter are shown in book x to be, as children are, even more impressionable than the adults. The precocious Kolya stands in for them in being divided between two opposed influences: that of the cynical materialist Rakitin, and Alyosha. Alyosha inspires in them the stout-hearted small fellowship commended by Zossima, which is unachieved by the adults.

Kolya is to accuse Alyosha of 'mysticism and obedience' (x.6), but this is a charge against which Dostoevsky early and notably defends him, calling him rather a realist (I.5). Although he acts promptly to save his father from Mitya's fury when the latter is kicking him in the face in a dress rehearsal for the murder, he is unable to heed Zossima's injunction to watch over Mitya, and help save him from himself. He is too distracted to do so, both by grief at Zossima's dying, and its manner, and by anguish at Ivan's assault on his faith.

If Alyosha is Zossima's spiritual son and heir, Mitya more clearly belongs to Karamazov. Both are seen as sensual clowns – and indeed Mitya identifies himself (VIII.5) with Yorick, the court jester from *Hamlet*. They share a temperament given over to appetite, although Mitya's is the more violent nature, and Karamazov's the more adept at satisfying financial greed.

Mitya is also the simpler and more child-like of the two; and, because of this, there is some truth in him, some real if undeveloped capacity for accurate self-assessment wholly lacking in his father. 'There's no order in me, no higher order' (vii.5) he is at least able to see.

'Beauty is a fearful and a terrifying thing! Fearful because it cannot be defined because God sets us nothing but riddles' (iii.3), Mitya tells Alyosha, and goes on to explain how maddened he feels that a man of great heart and high intelligence should begin with the ideal of the Madonna and end with the ideal of Sodom. In his own life these twin poles of 'sacred' and 'profane' love are played – or parodied – by the 'noble' Katerina and the 'fallen' Grushenka. Katerina's love for him, too, is double, infected by hurt pride over the humiliations she feels he has inflicted on her. Mitya's squandering of half the 3000 rubles she has entrusted to him to post for her proves his undoing. There is evidence he may have squandered the whole sum, whereas, unbeknown to the reader, he has sewn half of it into a rag which he wears around his neck. He twice hints at the existence of this 'amulet', but the reasons he stays quiet about it are typically two-sided. On the surface it is because, while he retains the 1500 rubles, he can persuade himself that he is not wholly without honour. His betrayal of Katerina's financial trust – perhaps, too, of her emotional trust – is not yet complete. And he is shown as obsessed by this moral indebtedness, approaching many different people to borrow the necessary sum and maddened by the loss of self-respect it entails, so that his violence during the tale owes something to this persistent wound he has created within his own self-esteem. At the same time he is also silent about the money because it represents a sum he could use to live off with Grushenka, should she consent to choose him rather than Karamazov. It represents, therefore, both the sacred and profane aspects of his moral life. By a characteristic Dostoevskian twist it is, however, Grushenka who is to prove most deeply loyal to him; while Katerina's histrionics, first on his behalf during the trial, and then in betraying him, ultimately help convict him.

The false trail laid by Dostoevsky to make the reader believe that Mitya is the murderer is an elaborate one. From book i onwards, the narrator associates the coming catastrophe with Mitya. In book ii he attacks his father verbally, and is singled

out by Zossima for suffering. In book III he attacks his father
physically, kicking him in the face. His desperate need for the
3000 rubles, precisely the sum that is to disappear from his
father's room at the time of the murder, is shown throughout.
And after the murder he mysteriously and suddenly possesses
money which he was formerly bereft of. The reader is not told
about the amulet containing Katerina's 1500 rubles until the
exact moment in the trial when the court-room learns of it.
There are other and detailed incriminating circumstances,
devilishly engineered by the cunning Smerdyakov, whose story
in book III is told with disingenuous apologies for detaining the
reader with a mere 'servant'. And Mitya has proclaimed that
he would rather be a murderer than fail to honour his debt to
Katerina (VIII.1), even writing to her in similar terms. He takes
a pestle on the night that his father is murdered, attacks
Grigory, and terrifies the servant Fenya.

Zossima had spoken of the only true punishment in this
world as that produced by the free action of conscience and
embraced by the self with humility. In this sense many of the
characters are engaged on moral pilgrimage, hurt and punished
by conscience, and Mitya foremost among them. He comes to
experience guilt, and to ready himself to embrace punishment,
not because he killed his father – he did not – but because he
certainly experienced the *desire* to do so, and because he has
lived thoughtlessly and violently, attacking such as Snegirov
and Grigory without cause or sense. Zossima, too, had suffered
his conversion as a young man after two acts of violence –
wantonly striking his batman, and challenging a fellow officer
of whom he was jealous to a duel. For Dostoevsky an active
sinner is closer to God and to a change of heart than a
lukewarm one, as in the parable from Revelation discussed by
Stepan Trofimovich at the end of *The Devils*, which prefers a
passionate to a mediocre sinner.

All three brothers are at least driven by passion. Alyosha's
passion is spiritual, Mitya's is sensual, and Ivan's intellectual.
Ivan experiences the temptations of the intellectual, living the
solitary life that Zossima fears, morose and withdrawn as a
child, friendless as an adult. His father comments that Ivan
loves nobody – 'He's not one of us' (II.2) – and his solitude is
emphasised throughout, not least by his name: he is the only
brother not referred to by an affectionate diminutive (Dmitri is

'Mitya', Alexander 'Alyosha'; for Ivan the equivalent would be 'Vanya').

The three middle chapters of book v, 'Pro and Contra', the most famous of the novel, are the centre of its idea-play. Here Ivan explains himself to Alyosha over fish soup, tea and jam, as they sit and talk in a bar – echoing Mitya's three chapters of confession to Alyosha in the orchard in book III.

In 'The Brothers Get Acquainted' Ivan explains that, despite his thirst for life and his joy in the 'sticky little green leaves that open up in the spring', he none the less fears the world's disorder, fears that the world may be no more than a 'disorderly, damnable and perhaps devil-ridden chaos'. He has learnt to love life more than the meaning of it, and advocates this position for others, loving life against 'logic'. After some talk of Katerina he addresses once more the 'eternal problems' and the question of what beliefs he lives by. He declares that he has an Euclidian (i.e. earth-bound) mind, baffled by the problem of the meeting of parallel lines in infinity: and baffled equally by the problems of disharmony and of evil, despite the promise held out by theologians of some 'ultimate' reconciliation.

He intensifies his attack in 'Rebellion', announcing that he will bring his arguments down to his despair, testing Alyosha's faith to the utmost, and partly wishing to be healed by Alyosha at the same time. For Ivan, as for the doctor cited by Zossima, love is a pretty but a theoretical ideal, impossible in reality. He comically cites the case of beggars presented in a ballet, wearing silken rags and tattered lace, begging for alms with grace. In reality and at close quarters – as opposed to such purely aesthetic daydreaming – the *details* of human need can often unmask compassion and altruism as forms of mere fantasy.

At this point Ivan begins his discourse on human suffering, restricting himself to the sufferings of children tortured or maltreated by adults. This picks up the discussion of children begun in 'Devout Peasant Women'. Ivan, like Dostoevsky himself, collects atrocity stories from the newspapers. A beast can never be as ingeniously, as *artistically* cruel as a man, he remarks. He notes a Turk who tossed and bayoneted a baby in front of its mother's eyes, and another who made a baby laugh before blowing out its brains. Turks, he adds mysteriously, are *very fond of sweets*. He tells of a wild man, Richard, a bastard child farmed out to and neglected by some peasants; he later,

partly in ignorance, robbed and killed, and then discovered
Christ and embraced suffering, but without his 'redemption'
preventing his cruel and needless execution. Ivan notes both
the obscenity of capital punishment and also how the pious
platitudes told of Richard's conversion should have made his
horrible death the more cruelly needless. Many human beings
procure a sensuous pleasure from cruelty, analogous, he implies,
to the Turks who are as fond of sweets as of sadism.

The terrible catalogue of horrors – which he sarcastically
calls 'charming pictures' – continues: a horse beaten across the
eyes and elegised by the poet Nekrassov, recalling Raskolnikov's
dream; a five-year-old girl shut up in mid-winter in an outdoor
privy, forced to eat her own excrement by her mother as a
punishment for bed-wetting. Just as parents torture their
children, so Ivan is aware of testing and torturing Alyosha
mentally, by this catalogue of horrors. The culmination of this
sequence is the story of a small boy who threw a stone in play
at, and hurt, the favourite hound of a general. The general had
the boy stripped and pursued by his hounds, who tore him
apart. Alyosha agrees with Ivan that this general, instead of
being merely deprived of the right to administer his estates,
should have been shot 'for the satisfaction of our moral feelings'.

In agreeing with Ivan, Alyosha has fallen into his trap.
Ivan's point is that suffering such as this cannot reasonably be
'atoned for' or made right. Ivan hungers for signs of a divine
justice that might reconcile him to existence, but simultaneously
rejects a world in which the price of such 'ultimate' harmony
could be the degradation and torture of children. 'Too high a
price has been placed on harmony. We cannot afford to pay so
much for admission' into some supposed future Elysium. When
Alyosha protests that this is 'rebellion' on Ivan's part – linking
him, by implication, with a Luciferian pride – Ivan challenges
him to imagine that *he*, Alyosha, were creating the world anew,
and that he found that universal peace and contentment could
be purchased at the cost of the torture to death of just *one* such
child: would Alyosha consent to be the cosmic architect under
such conditions? He would not, he agrees.

Ivan's complaint explicitly recalls the lamentations of the
devout peasant woman consoled by Zossima in book II, who
was told to make a healing surrender to God and time, to cure
her grief for her dead child (see Jackson, 1981, ch. 14). Ivan,

unlike this mother, refuses to cease the work of mourning. He hungers for a miracle before making any gesture of faithful assent to the world; he would also reject a miracle purchased at the cost of such suffering if one occurred.

The reason why Ivan's case has such power is that it is irrefutable. His heartless questioning of the conditions of existence represents one kind of truth. Zossima's wisdom simply represents another. Neither case can 'win', and nor can the conflict between them be resolved intellectually. The test is that, while both points of view can be inhabited and lived by, Ivan's is, by definition, a commitment to bitter and lonely suffering, Zossima's to the principle of renewal in human life. Like Euclidian and post-Euclidian geometry, each has its own internal coherence. The war between them reflects the embattled vision of the soul that the novel insists on throughout, with its repeated picture of its protagonists struggling from 'darkness' towards, or away from, 'light'; hence the title of book v, 'Pro and Contra', for and against, which has the widest possible reference. The positive element that Alyosha suggests Ivan may have left out of account is the life of Christ, and it is to the significance of Christ's mission that Ivan now turns, in 'The Grand Inquisitor', a poem, as he terms it, that he once wrote and which Alyosha here in the bar will be the first to hear. Set in Seville during the terrible years of the Inquisition, it concerns a Second Coming of Christ, who is recognised and besought to perform miracles. This he starts to do, when the Grand Inquisitor, an old man of nearly ninety, tall and erect with shrivelled face and sunken eyes, sees and detains him and announces that tomorrow he will burn him at the stake as 'the vilest of heretics'. The bulk of the 'poem' concerns his speech to the silent Christ explaining his reasons for condemning him.

His chief charge against Christ is that Christ has exaggerated man's capacity to bear the agonies of free will. Christ came to liberate men from the rigours of the old law, and to persuade them to choose good of their own accord. But, argues the Grand Inquisitor, most people are no more than rebellious slaves, who would be maddened by free choice if granted it. Only the Few are capable of truly suffering such choice. Christ rejected his temptations in the wilderness in the name of freedom. He refused to purchase belief through miracle, because that would have deprived men of the right to choose freely. But most of humanity want nothing better than to yield up the burden of free will, and they long to surrender to power. Therefore the 'miracle, mystery and authority' rejected by Christ in the wilderness, and on the cross, are enshrined in and exploited by the Catholic Church, for the good of the Many, who do not know, and need to have explained, what is best for them. Left to their own devices, they would eat one another alive.

Alyosha at once sees that this parable is an attack on the Roman Catholic Church, which Dostoevsky represents as a State arrogating to itself churchly privilege, rather than that true Church within which the State might wither away. This dichotomy Ivan had already (ambiguously) described in his essay that is discussed in book II, 'It will be! It will be!' And much of the power of Dostoevsky's portrait of Ivan comes from the fact that his is a spiritual struggle. Alyosha believes that Ivan seeks suffering (II.7); Zossima speaks of Ivan's 'pilgrimage' towards 'higher things' (II.6).

Ivan's parable draws some of its force from its development of one of Dostoevsky's continuing nightmares. The vision of a future world divided between an amoral 'Few' and an enslaved 'Many' recurs in novel after novel. In *Crime and Punishment* Raskolnikov uses this vision as a specious excuse for murder, testing out his membership of the elite. In *The Devils* Shigalyov's vision is of a stultified utopia where the Many suffer for eternity, pawns of a devilish boss–class. Here Ivan is not, of course, advocating this nightmare future. It is rather that he can find no force adequate to the task of refuting it. And his guilt lies both in his intellectual apostasy, and also in the effect that his lack of beliefs has on others. Christ's reaction to the Grand Inquisitor was to kiss him on his 'bloodless, aged lips'. Alyosha kisses Ivan too, but is clearly disturbed.

There is an ambiguity as to whether Ivan believes that from now on 'All is permitted' or, rather, 'All is enjoined' – even cannibalism – as is more than once suggested. When Lise tells him of her obscenely cruel fantasy of watching a small child being crucified while eating pineapple compote, he is reported as laughing ambiguously. 'That is good' (XI.3). He often speaks with a cynical complaisance about evil-doing. On Mitya's first assault on their father, he observes that 'One reptile will devour another and serve them both right' (III.9), and later echoes the fratricide Cain when Alyosha seeks Mitya's whereabouts: 'I am not my brother's keeper' (v.3). The dramatic power and intensity of his three interviews with Smerdyakov depend upon Smerdyakov – who plays double or monster to Ivan's Frankenstein – gradually forcing Ivan deeper and deeper into an awareness of his own half-conscious assent to his father's murder, and thus to his complicity in it. 'I was only your apprentice, your loyal page, and I done it because you told me to' (xi.8), Smerdyakov finally tells him. Much given to blasphemous casuistry, Smerdyakov takes Ivan's 'All is permitted' as a new anti-Gospel which he then deliberately acts out. In this sense Karamazov may have been right when he twice speaks of Ivan, rather than Dmitri, as the son from whom he had most to fear (iii.9, iv.2).

Ivan's discovery of his own guilt is at once followed by his waking nightmare of meeting the Devil as a down-at-heels but worldly gentleman, given to facetious jokes, who tells him that hell has adopted the new metric system and that he longs to be reincarnated as the fat, sixteen-stone wife of a merchant. He represents the 'indispensable minus sign' in the world. His is the necessary negation without which, he nastily suggests, Christ's positives would have no work to do. 'If everything on earth were rational, nothing would happen.' Through his agency, God's Hosannahs are 'tried in the crucible of doubt'. If all the world were entirely light, or entirely dark, there would be nothing to see by. But this Devil equivocates about everything: about whether or not Ivan is dreaming, whether or not God exists, whether or not faith or doubt are most appropriate. On waking, Ivan learns that Smerdyakov – on whose testimony Mitya's salvation depends – has hanged himself. And, overwhelmed by a new apprehension of his own guilt, and yet lacking any spiritual machinery by which this guilt might be put either to work or to rest, Ivan goes mad, and thus spoils his own intervention on Mitya's behalf at the trial.

Smerdyakov is not the only person influenced by Ivan. Alyosha is so bemused that he neglects to keep a watchful eye on Mitya, who in his turn is also much struck by Ivan's views. A peasant woman at the start of the novel had asked Zossima for shriving for the very *thought* of murder (ii.3). In this novel the author's great moral searching-out of his characters is conducted, not simply as behaviourists and existentialists would have it, through their deeds, but through the moment-to-moment quality of their thought and belief. As Hingley satirically puts this, 'Smerdyakov was the least guilty; he merely committed [the murder]' (1962, p. 200). As readers we are implicated, too, in the communal guilt when Ivan cries out to the court-room, 'Who doesn't wish his father dead? . . . The liars! They all wish their father dead' (xii.5). Thus Ivan is maddened by his inability either to forget the suffering of others, or his own complicity; while Mitya is to begin to learn to embrace unmerited suffering with a full and open heart, and conscious ownership. Where Ivan dreams of the Devil, and Alyosha dreams of Christ and Zossima, Mitya's pivotal dream occurs during his interrogation and concerns, once more, the suffering of children.

He dreams of a burnt-out village in the Steppes, with haggard peasants and a baby crying from the cold. 'Why are people poor? Why's the "babby" poor? Why's the steppe so bare? Why don't they embrace and kiss one another?' (ix.8) asks Mitya in his dream, in a sequence that moves from Ivan's heartless questioning of terrible suffering towards a joyous, personal acceptance. A dream-Grushenka appears and promises never to cease loving him, or desert him, and he wakes, in wonder and humility, marvelling that some unknown person has supported his sleeping head with a pillow. 'I've had a good dream, gentlemen!' he tells his interrogators, his face transformed and radiant with joy. From this moment he starts to accept his fate with a brave absence of self-pity, able to rest in the tormenting compassion to be felt for all suffering humanity.

Grushenka, too, is changed by suffering. She had been seduced by a Pole, and had evolved a dramatic life-myth of unappeased and unaccepted pain, which makes her capricious and unreliable. She pretends (like Nastasya) to be sexually promiscuous when she is not. And, when she remeets her seducer at Mikroye, he turns out to be an unprepossessing little fat Pole with a pipe, a very cheap wig, dyed moustaches, a pompous humourless card-sharp who later importunes her for 2000 rubles, but drops, by degrees, to the demand for a single ruble. Mitya, to his own slow amazement, has no problem rescuing her from this buffoon, and her new, absolute commitment to him and to the suffering in store for both of them procures for her a new seriousness.

What chiefly dogs a true redemptive suffering, throughout Dostoevsky, is the perverse parody of it to be found in the ultimately sensual longing to inflict or receive pain. Here sado-masochism is to be found in the many stories of beating and flogging, and in the 'little she-devil', the crippled Lise Khokhlakov, who, after recounting her grotesque fantasy of watching the crucifying child while eating stewed pineapple, smashes her finger in the door, murmuring, 'Mean, mean!'

A more secretive and devious, but no less damaging variety of sado-masochistic feeling is to be found in Katerina, who continues throughout the story to swing between a proud self-surrender and an equally assertive self-will. In her the capacity of the self-assertive will to parody self-effacement is seen to be fathomless. At the trial she first sacrifices her reputation to save Mitya and then, stung by Ivan's testimony and hysterical, damages Mitya's case catastrophically by producing his incriminating letter to her.

The whole burden of Zossima's – and of Dostoevsky's – case is that moral regeneration must be embraced wholeheartedly by the individual free will. State punishment, which Dostoevsky had undergone, and which is now in store for Mitya, represents a grotesque parody of this process, the more so here in that Mitya is not a parricide. So, once Mitya is convicted, a scheme is afoot to bribe the guards and rescue him, taking him to America – a fate, throughout Dostoevsky, quite as awful as Siberia. There Mitya will suffer a purging homesickness, and return with Grushenka, with a new *incognito*.

The book ends with little Ilyusha's funeral. Alyosha exhorts the school-fellows who mourn Ilyusha's death always to cherish such good memories as will help them in their own battles between the darkness and the light. The precocious young rationalist Kolya is moved to lead the round of applause which, in a coda both sentimental and very moving, ends the novel.

7
Conclusion

The question of Dostoevsky's 'modernity' might be opened by comparing him with Dickens. As is often pointed out, the two are similar and yet different. In neither is the presentation of women really satisfactory. We get she-devils (especially in Dostoevsky) and comic matriarchs, both of whom partly exist in order to dramatise the predicaments of the male characters. Nature is painted in only a desultory fashion, especially in Dostoevsky. There is an idealisation and cult of the child in both writers as Romantic innocent and as symbol of future hope. Both attack utilitarianism and scientific rationalism, notably in *Hard Times* and in *Crime and Punishment* and *Notes from Underground*. And yet we feel flattered by Dostoevsky's greater closeness to us in – to take one example – his eschewing of a 'moralised' use of death-bed scenes. Compare the deaths of Jo in *Bleak House*, or of Carker in *Dombey and Son*, with that of the Marmeladov parents in *Crime and Punishment*. Despite the developed taste both had for *Grand Guignol*, and their love of reading about or visiting scenes of horror, dying in Dickens has a much clearer moral or rhetorical function. In Dostoevsky, we feel tempted to say, it simply happens, and often engenders in us contradictory and confusing responses, closer to the messiness of emotion in real life. Dostoevsky's refusal of the simply-tragic nourishes that of many present-day writers, for whom a tragic vision can also be expressed through a partly comic or ironic form.

The influence of so great a writer as Dostoevsky is hard to pin down. It affects the very way we perceive. In the case of lesser writers, the question of 'influence' can be set forth in a more pedestrian spirit. Dostoevsky's influence, for example, has been detected in the work of – among others – Thomas Mann, André Gide, T. S. Eliot, Aldous Huxley, Somerset Maugham,

William Faulkner, Hugh Walpole, Samuel Beckett, Max Frisch, Joseph Conrad and D. H. Lawrence. And the last two of these writers both disliked and suspected Dostoevsky.

The use made of Dostoevsky by writers of the first half of this century has been discussed elsewhere (Muchnic, 1962; see also Wellek, 1962, pp. 1–15). I shall restrict this very brief discussion of Dostoevsky's 'modernity' to a few perceptions of his work: that it is uniquely open to interpretation; that he presents a giddy, destabilised world; and that his work seems to 'prophesy the twentieth century'. I shall then move to a contemporary writer in whom Dostoevsky's influence is very much alive, though hitherto little remarked.

To deal with the least interesting claim first: Dostoevsky's work seems to prophesy modern terrorism and totalitarianism (for example, in *The Devils*), the replacement of religion by science, and the deification of man in place of God (as in the existentialists, for instance). If this is so, it is naturally because terrorism, atheism and so forth made their mark on the nineteenth century, and Dostoevsky was simply more deeply in touch with his own time than many of his contemporaries. Within his time the seeds of our own are of course to be found. Indeed, Russia in the 1860s, with its feminism, its cranky utopianisms by the dozen, its violent instability and threat of terrorism, its desperate hunger for and fear of 'the new', sometimes looks like a dress rehearsal for the twentieth century. It is the place and period in which many modern anxieties were born, the crucible of much contemporary doubt. Most of its intellectual decor had recently arrived from the West, but in Russia was given a strange impetus and intensity which belonged peculiarly to the Russian situation. The very word 'intelligentsia' comes to us out of this Russia, and the alienation and bitter self-division of the Russian intelligentsia speak directly to our own.

As for the self-flattering desire that art should be a source of prophecy about our own troubles, this comes to us direct, of course, from Romanticism. Our sense of crisis, our whole fetishistic cult of 'modernity', with its special pleading about the present, is Romantic. D. S. Mirsky excellently wrote fifty years ago (in his preface to Carr, 1931) that 'much that seems modern in Dostoevsky is modern only in so far as the term "modern" can be extended to Rousseau, Byron and Benjamin

Constant. . . . If he was accepted as modern by intellectuals of twentieth-century Europe, it was because Europe herself had entered a *seconde jeunesse* of neo-Romanticism.' These words – including the caveat about contemporary Romanticism – seem no less true today than they were in 1931. Some of Dostoevsky's current influence has to do with our own neurotic cult of apocalypse and crisis, which can feel directly addressed by the cult of intensity to be found in 1860s' Russia. What nineteenth-century hero is as Byronic and backword-looking as Stavrogin – and, at the same time, as forward-looking, standing, together with Ivan Karamazov and Kirilov, behind Albert Camus in *The Rebel* (1951) and *The Outsider* (1942)?

Throughout his work Dostoevsky attacks the vision of an enslaved and determined majority ruled over by a liberated elite. And he similarly attacks the vision of a determined present yoked to a wholly emancipated future. This unique and heady marriage of determinism-with-idealism was to be found, in his own day, in that handbook for contemporary radicals, Chernyshevsky's *What is to be Done?*, which combines a pseudo-scientific behaviourism with a facile utopian view of the future. It is a Romantic vision, for all its apparently unillusioned 'realism'. Dostoevsky attacks it in the name of an essentially spiritual soul-picture: the redemption he seeks is religious.

Recent modish 'progressive' French theories of various kinds – both existentialism and its direct heir, structuralism – inherited exactly this view of *ordinary* people as merely the victims of bourgeois conditioning, and of the *intellectual* as possessing the magical freedom to modify the self as realm of pure possibility. The common man is a mere passive rendezvous of codes, unaware that he is *spoken by* language, while the theoretician is a kind of poet levitating outside the borders of language, manufacturing new concepts.[18] 'An irresponsible and undirected self-assertion . . . goes hand-in-hand with some brand of pseudo-scientific determinism. . . . *An unexamined sense of the strength of the machine is combined with the illusion of jumping out of it.*'[19]

Dostoevsky militates against this marriage of determinism-with-idealism throughout his work. His is a twin-pronged attack, which emphasises both that we are uglier than we pretend and that we are more spiritually redeemable than we dare allow. He defends a religious soul-picture against the new scientific rationalism. It is little wonder that D. H.

Lawrence calls Dostoevsky's characters – with scorn – 'fallen angels'.

In religion Dostoevsky belonged to the old order, in psychology to the new (see Carr, 1931, p. 323). Until recently, it has been his psychology that writers have inherited, rather than his spiritual claims. This has made for a lop-sided view, but one which marks writer after writer in whom his influence might be discerned. They emphasise our 'fallenness', irrationality and inner darkness, rather than our capacity for moral change or redeemability. And Dostoevsky's emphasis on our self-contradiction and dark irrationality, his immense and uncanny psychological penetration by itself, bereft of hope of or belief in change – except of an instantaneous, utopian and unreal kind – produces merely a stale sentimental pessimism. Such a sentimentality of darkness seems no more edifying than the sentimentality of light purveyed by minor writers a century ago. The vulgar interest in perverse psychology for its own sake, such as can be found, for instance, in Ian McEwan or Martin Amis, who could be said to use a Dostoevskian Gothic, often reads as equivalent to that special hypocrisy of boasting that one is nastier than one really is, which Dostoevsky devastatingly analyses in his fiction.

Dostoevsky bequeathes us a giddy, destabilised view of the world, which appeals to our special passion for knowing the worst. He also leaves us a novel-form uniquely able to do what Samuel Beckett argued is the special task of art in our century: to accommodate mess or contingency, while still remaining art.[20] Dostoevsky loves to depict those experiences that destabilise the soul, and the effect of his turbulent aesthetics is to drive us hard into *impasse*: again and again, we suffer both a low craving for sensation and a vain hope of redemption, in an impossible tension. The comedy, oddly enough, never *anaesthetises* us against such irreducible *aporia*, but unsettles and perplexes us further.

And his influence, indeed, is still widespread. J. G. Farrell's character of Sarah Devlin in his magnificent *Troubles* (1970), an Irish semi-cripple with an urge to be dominated by a man even more violent and perverse than she is, surely owes almost everything to Lise Khokhlakov in *The Brothers Karamazov*. Angus Wilson's Arthur Calvert in *Late Call* (1964), a tall-story teller of a special kind, has one fictional origin in General Ivolgin – just as the scene in which Hamo Langmuir smashes Zoe's

Nymphenburg harlequin in Wilson's later *As if by Magic* (1973) is a clear homage to Myshkin's breaking of the Chinese vase in *The Idiot*. Even our apparently new, and so typically 'mid-century' sub-genre, the 'campus novel', could be said to have a Dostoevskian provenance. Randall Jarrell's *Pictures from an Institution* (1954), Mary McCarthy's *The Groves of Academe* (1952), Malcolm Bradbury's *Eating People is Wrong* (1959), *Stepping Westwards* (1965) and *The History Man* (1975), and David Lodge's *Changing Places* (1975) may have one parochial source in the tradition of novel-of-ideas as developed through Thomas Love Peacock, W. H. Mallock and Aldous Huxley. But they surely owe another debt to *The Devils*, a novel whose attack on progressive pieties makes our own look paltry, for its depiction of a more savage collision of airy idealism with a pedestrian or ugly reality in a closed community.

If one had to choose a single writer today in whom Dostoevsky's influence is most digested and most fruitful, it would surely be Iris Murdoch. She shares much with him, and yet makes a purely distinctive fictional world of her own. As far back as her first novel, *Under the Net* (1954), she presented a character, Hugo Belfounder, who is akin to Prince Myshkin. Both Hugo and Myshkin are absurd, impractical patrician spiritual seekers with a gift for renunciation, who have a large effect on everyone whom they meet. And Murdoch's second novel, *The Flight from the Enchanter* (1956), contains both a classic *skandal* scene, in Mischa's disastrous grand party, and a strictly Dostoevskian use of a 'double', where the unhappy Calvin Blick is the agent of all Mischa Fox's worst designs, and embodies and makes visible his unconscious. Both Murdoch and Dostoevsky have directly addressed the problems of creating characters who are good – difficult in any age, and requiring special courage in our own. Myshkin haunts a number of Murdoch's virtuous characters – for example, the Christ-like Tallis in *A Fairly Honourable Defeat* (1970), who shares his epilepsy, his awkward foolishness, his sense of being out of focus with ordinary appetite.

And yet what is interesting about both writers is how they use their art not simply for missionary purposes, but to test out their own best beliefs. Their good characters have to take their chance in the maelstrom of the plot, together with everyone else. Both are haunted by Christ as an ethical ideal, and both have a quarrel with God the Father, a doubleness that gives their novels a special sense of risk and freedom. The most iconoclastic of Dostoevsky's narrators, the Underground Man, is echoed by Bradley Pearson in *The Black Prince* (1973) and by Hilary Burde in *A Word Child* (1974), who share his subversive intimacy with the reader and his indecent exposure of consciousness. That 'all is permitted' runs as a slogan throughout Iris Murdoch's work, just as much as it does through Dostoevsky's, energising the plots and used by her characters as an excuse for moral carelessness and depravity.

In *A Severed Head* (1961) Martin Lynch-Gibbon is tempted by the demonic Palmer Anderson into a *ménage-à-trois* with his half-sister Honor Klein, with whom he is having an incestuous relationship. 'On the whole, "do what you want" costs others less than "do what you ought" ', he argues (Penguin edn, p. 167); and Martin reflects that never has he heard speak more clearly the voice that says, 'All is permitted'.

That 'all is permitted' was the preoccupying thought of Raskolnikov and of Ivan Karamazov. In *The Devils* the nihilists act it out. It is the source of energy in plot after plot of Dostoevsky, associated with murder in all four of the great novels, and with child-abuse or rape in three. That 'all is permitted' is a fear that also haunts Rozanov in Iris Murdoch's recent *The Philosopher's Pupil* (1983), the most openly Dostoevskian of all her novels. Here Rozanov's self-appointed pupil George, who is also Rozanov's 'double' in a strict Dostoevskian sense, wants to act the slogan out. In a letter to Rozanov he associates the idea of getting beyond good and evil not with Nietzsche, but with Dostoevsky (Chatto edn, p. 415). The cruelty and capriciousness that are frozen in Rozanov are openly displayed in the demonic George, who acts out his iconoclasm, smashing up some priceless Roman glass and attempting to murder both his wife and Rozanov himself. In this latter attempt on his own father-figure he echoes the parricide of *The Brothers Karamazov*. And *The Philosopher's Pupil* shares with that novel, too, three brothers, one innocent (Tom), one bad but redeemable (George) who combines features of both Ivan and Mitya while differing from both, and one merely mediocre (Brian). The narrative technique, moreover, borrows directly from *The Devils*, with its fussy, gossiping narrator, half in, half out of the story, sometimes accurate and reliable, sometimes lapsing into rumour and uncertainty.

Both Murdoch and Dostoevsky associate the slogan 'all is permitted' with total moral shamelessness and ethical solipsism. Both see the present age as in a spiritual crisis following on from the collapse of religious dogma, a crisis charted by Dostoevsky in *The Devils* and echoed by Murdoch in *The Time of the Angels* (1967) in particular. Her 'angels' turn out to be demonic too. The importance of this last book is underlined when its title is discussed, nearly twenty years later, in *The Philosopher's Pupil*, where Rozanov speaks of 'the problem of our age, our interregnum, our interim, our time of the angels'. 'Why angels?' asks Jacoby. 'Spirit without God', says Rozanov (p.187).

In the fallen world that both writers present, their characters chiefly communicate through past wounds. They may aim at altruism, but often achieve something closer to sado-masochism. In both, the self-assertive will endlessly parodies a true self-effacement, and the temptation to pass on a hurt to others is seldom resisted; or the hurt is internalised by the good self punishing the bad self and enjoying its own humiliation in a proud self-abasement. In *Crime and Punishment* Dostoevsky writes, after the street accident that kills Marmeladov, of the secret satisfaction that even a truly altruistic person may experience at a disaster; while in *The Philosopher's Pupil* the narrator describes the curious elation survivors can feel after a funeral.

For both writers, art is thus a playground or battleground for unconscious forces. And both have been charged with writing 'unrealism' and have (properly) defended themselves on the ground that they are in fact writing a 'deeper' realism. Two features stand out here. One is the shared use of compressed time-schemes, the other the use of 'scandals'. To Strakhov Dostoevsky wrote that he had his own view of art and that that which the majority call fantastic and exceptional was for him the very essence of reality (*Letters*, 10 March 1869). The first, most successful book of *The Idiot* is jam-packed with sensational incident and coincidence, and later sections never quite recapture its hectic brilliance. Dostoevsky's fictional imagination works best in short, compressed bands of time. So does Iris Murdoch's. Many of her novels occupy, like *Crime and Punishment*, less than two weeks. These are exciting, sensational plots, employing chance and coincidence with a magnificent bravura, owing much to the Gothic tradition.

Murdoch also inherits Dostoevsky's use of scandal or set-piece fiasco scenes, from Rosa's hurling of the paperweight at the fishbowl at Mischa's grand party in *The Flight from the Enchanter* (1956) – in the attempt to save the goldfish, one gets dropped by mistake into a decanter of gin – to the riotous party in the Slipper House in *The Philosopher's Pupil*.

A Severed Head and *A Fairly Honourable Defeat* are structured entirely in terms of broken feasts or parties, in small scenes of acute embarrassment and distress which unmask private pain. No writer is more embarrassing – that is, raises embarrassment to a higher, more poetic art – than Dostoevsky. In this, if in nothing else, Murdoch is his direct heir. Embarrassment links with humour, which both use to display the sheer, irrational confusion of life. We laugh at the affront to our own fastidiousness, at the horrible clowning that draws us steadily into acknowledging membership of a community of fools. Both intermingle farce and tragedy which an apparent callousness. 'Humour is the wit of deep feeling', wrote Dostoevsky (*The Diary of a Writer*, March 1877, III.2) in considering the problems of describing a scene of painful squalor. Murdoch has consistently admired Dostoevsky as a *comic* writer,[21] and one function of the comedy in both is to drive us hard against the intractable *detail* of lives other than our own, in all their glorious, embarrassing, painful absurdity. Comedy relates to the delight both feel in the sheer irreducibility of their own characters.

And, finally, both use art to test out their own pieties. The devils often have the best tunes. 'Purging God's Hosannahs in the crucible of doubt' was how Ivan's Devil expressed the process in *The Brothers Karamazov*. In *A Severed Head* the demon Palmer Anderson's description of the psyche as essentially mechanical (p. 30) comes closer to an accurate description of the plot of lovers-on-the-rebound than anyone else. In *The Time of the Angels* the mad and bad Carel's vision of the negative sublime, of cosmic chaos, is also the closest we get to the truth of that book. And in *A Fairly Honourable Defeat* the Grand Inquisitor Julius King brilliantly and accurately describes human behaviour in the grip of or enslaved to the unconscious mind when he calls human beings 'essentially finders of substitutes' who never really see one another at all. 'Anyone will do to play the roles . . .' (Penguin edn, p. 233). This is not to say, naturally, that either Dostoevsky or Murdoch wholly agrees with such demonic voices. But the final word, which would judge and 'place' them, is deliberately left unspoken.

It has been unjustly said of both these writers that they advocate suffering for its own sake. In fact, 'the positive message of Myshkin, Stepan Trofimovich, Zossima, is that man is born for happiness' (Peace, 1971, p. 306); while Murdoch has praised happiness as a force for good both within and outside her fiction. 'The books are full of happiness. . . . I feel they are *shining* with happiness', she has said.[22]

In a letter about *Poor Folk* (1 February 1846) Dostoevsky claimed, with justifiable pride, that he had not 'exposed his ugly mug' within his fiction. If it is uniquely true of those writers whom we like to term 'modern' that their work comes to us without the guarantee provided by an authorial 'personality' or 'voice', then it is also true of all great writers in every age that their authors remain in some sense invisible within them. This, perhaps, is the only sense in which 'modernity' can be finally meaningful: that the works we praise by calling modern are built to last, are perennially fresh, alive and untamable.

Notes

1. John Bayley, *Tolstoi and the Novel* (London: Chatto and Windus, 1968) p. 184.

2. Sigmund Freud, 'Dostoevsky and Parricide', collected in Wellek (1962) pp. 98–111.

3. There is now some debate as to whether Dostoevsky said this. See S. A. Reiser in *Poetika i stilistika russkoi literaturi* (1971) pp. 187–9; and J. Jones (1983) p. 31.

4. For a fuller discussion, see Peace (1971) pp. 33–4; and N. A. Dobrolyubov, *Selected Philosophical Essays*, tr. J. Fineberg (Moscow: Foreign Languages Publishing House, 1956) p. 375.

5. Lionel Trilling, *Beyond Culture* (Harmondsworth: Penguin, 1967) pp. 36–7; J. Bayley, 'Character and Consciousness', *New Literary History*, v (Winter 1974) 225–35.

6. Unless it be the hatred of older gentry-intelligentsia for those 1950s *raznochintsy*, the 'Angry Young Men'. For Somerset Maugham's furious reaction to Kingsley Amis's *Lucky Jim*, for example, see R. Rabinowitz, *The Reaction against Experiment in the English Novel* (Novel York: Columbia University Press, 1967).

7. Bayley, *Tolstoi and the Novel*, p. 184.

8. For Freud on Dostoevsky, see Joseph Frank's *Dostoevsky*, especially vol. 1 (1977).

9. De Quincey, 'On the Knocking on the Gate in *Macbeth*', in *Shakespeare, a Biography* (Edinburgh: A. & C. Black, 1864) pp. 85–91.

10. I regret that shortage of space has obliged me to simplify my account of the role of the narrator. For a full examination of the unreliability of the narrator, see Miller (1981).

11. Lev Shestov, 'The Gift of Prophecy', in *Anton Chehov and Other Essays*, tr. S. Koteliansky (Dublin: Maunsell, 1916) p. 78.

12. Ronald Hingley writes about the formal characteristics of scandal scenes throughout *The Undiscovered Dostoevsky* (1962).

13. M. Krieger, 'Dostoevsky's "Idiot": The Curse of Saintliness', in *The Tragic Vision* (New York: Holt, Reinhart and Winston, 1960) pp. 209–27, collected in Wellek (1962) pp. 39–52.

14. See, for example, Albert Camus, *Myth of Sisyphus*, tr. J. O'Brien (London: Hamish Hamilton, 1942).

15. For further elaboration of these points, see Peace (1971) pp. 218ff.

16. T. S. Eliot, *Selected Essays* (1932), collected in *Tennyson's 'In Memoriam'*, ed. J. .D Hunt (London: Macmillan, 1970) pp. 135.

17. I gratefully owe this formulation of Zossima's message to Professor Belknap in 'Dostoevsky's Last Inspirational Speeches: A Rhetorical Study', a paper given at the Sixth International Dostoevsky Symposium in Nottingham, 1986.

18. See Peter Conradi, '3 Critics and the Sublime', *Critical Quarterly*, XXVII, no. 1 (Spring, 1985) 25–42.

19. Iris Murdoch, *The Sovereignty of Good* (London: Routledge and Kegan Paul, 1970) p. 48 [my emphasis].

20. Cited in B. S. Johnson's introduction to *Aren't You Rather Young to be Writing Your Memoirs?* (London: Hutchinson, 1973), collected in Malcolm Bradbury (ed.), *The Novel Today* (Glasgow: Collins, 1977) p. 156.

21. 'A novel is a comic form. A novel that isn't at all comic is [in] great danger, aesthetically speaking, that is ... my God how comic, for instance, Dostoevsky is, frightfully funny ...' – in H. Ziegler and C. Bigsby (eds), *The Radical Imagination and the Liberal Tradition: Interviews with Novelists* (London: Junction Books, 1982).

22. In John Haffenden (ed.), *Novelists in Interview* (London and New York: Methuen) p. 204. Some of these ideas are developed further in Peter Conradi, *Iris Murdoch: The Saint and the Artist* (London: Macmillan; New York: St Martin's Press, 1988, 2nd edn), and 'Dostoevsky and Iris Murdoch', in R. Todd (ed.), *Encounter with Iris Murdoch* (Amsterdam: Free University of Amsterdam Press, 1987).

Select Bibliography

What follows is merely a minute selection from the materials available in English. Serious students of Dostoevsky are recommended to turn to the journal *Dostoevsky Studies*, to the bulletin of the International Dostoevsky Society, and to the Dostoevsky entries in Garth Terry's three volumes of *East European Languages and Literatures*. Vol. I (1900–77) was published by Clio Press, Oxford, in 1978; vols II (1978–81) and III (1982–4) were each published by Astra Press, Nottingham, in 1982 and 1985 respectively. In Garth Terry and Malcolm Jones (eds), *New Essays on Dostoevsky* (Cambridge: Cambridge University Press, 1983) pp. 215–48 contains a most useful survey of Dostoevsky studies in Great Britain, while pp. 215–19 give a wealth of information about other sources.

PRIMARY SOURCES

1846	*Poor Folk*
	The Double
1840	*Netotchka Nezvanova*
1861	*The House of the Dead*
	The Insulted and the Injured
1862	*Winter Notes on Summer Impressions*
1864	*Notes from Underground*
1866	*The Gambler*
	Crime and Punishment
1868	*The Idiot*
1870	*The Eternal Husband*
1871	*The Devils*; [*Stavrogin's Confession* (the banned chapter), tr. S. Koteliansky and V. Woolf (London: Hogarth Press, 1922)]
1875	*A Raw Youth*
1877	*The Dream of a Ridiculous Man*
1880	*The Brothers Karamazov*

1873, 1876–7, 1880, 1881: *The Diary of a Writer*, tr. B. Brasol, 2 vols (Cassell, 1951).
Pisma (Letters), 4 vols, ed. A. Dolinin (Moscow–Leningrad, 1922–8), selections of which have been published in, for example, *Dostoevsky: A Self-Portrait*, ed. and tr. J. Coulson (Oxford: Oxford University Press, 1962); *Letters of F. M. Dostoevsky to his Family and Friends*, tr. E. C. Mayne (London: Chatto and Windus, 1917); and *New Dostoevsky Letters*, tr. S. Koteliansky (London: Mandrake, 1929).

SECONDARY SOURCES

An asterisk (*) after an entry indicates that the book contains a useful bibliography.

Bakhtin, Mikhail M., *Problems of Dostoevsky's Poetics*, ed. and tr. C. Emerson (Manchester: Manchester University Press, 1984).
Belknap, Robert L., *The Structure of 'The Brothers Karamazov'* (The Hague and Paris: Mouton, 1967).
Berdyaev, Nicholas, *Dostoevsky*, tr. D. Attwater (New York: Meridian, 1957).
Busch, Robert L., *Humor in the Major Novels of Dostoevsky* (Slavica, forthcoming).*
Carr, Edward H., *Dostoevsky: A New Biography* (London: Allen and Unwin, 1931).
Catteau, Jacques, *La Création littéraire chez Dostoevski*, translation to be published by Cambridge University Press.
Dostoyevsky, Aimee, *Fyodor Dostoyevsky: A Study* (London: Heinemann, 1921).
Dostoyevsky, Anna, *Dostoyevsky: Reminiscences* (London: Wildwood House, 1976).
Eng, J. van der, and Meijer, J. M., *'The Brothers Karamazov': Essays* (The Hague and Paris: Mouton, 1971).
Frank, Joseph, *Dostoevsky: The Seeds of Revolt (1821–1849)* (London: Robson; and Princeton, NJ: Princeton University Press, 1977).
——, *Dostoevsky: The Years of Ordeal (1850–1859)* (London: Robson; and Princeton, NJ: Princeton University Press, 1983).
——, *Dostoevsky: The Stir of Liberation (1860–1865)* (Princeton, NJ: Princeton University Press, 1986). (Further volumes awaited.)
Freeborn, Richard, *The Rise of the Russian Novel* (Cambridge: Cambridge University Press, 1973).
Gibson, A. Boyce, *The Religion of Dostoevsky* (London: SCM Press, 1973).
Gide, André, *Dostoevsky*, tr. and introd. Arnold Bennett (London: J. M. Dent, 1925).
Goldstein, David, *Dostoyevsky and the Jews* (Austin and London: Texas University Press, 1981).
Grossman, Leonid G., *Dostoevsky: A Biography*, tr. Mary Mackler (London: Allen Lane, 1974).
Hingley, Ronald, *The Undiscovered Dostoyevsky* (London: Hamish Hamilton, 1962).
Howe, Irving, 'The Politics of Salvation', in *Politics and the Novel* (London: Stevens, 1961).

Jackson, Robert L., *Dostoevsky's Underground Man in Russian Literature* (The Hague: Mouton, 1958).

——, *Dostoevsky's Quest for Form* (New Haven, Conn., and London: Yale University Press, 1966).

—— (ed.), *Twentieth Century Interpretations of 'Crime and Punishment'* (Englewood Cliffs, NJ: Prentice-Hall, 1974).

——, *The Art of Dostoevsky* (Princeton, Princeton University Press, 1981).

——, *New Perspectives* (Englewood Cliffs, NJ: Prentice-Hall, 1984).

Jones, John, *Dostoevsky* (Oxford and New York: Oxford University Press, 1983).

Jones, Malcolm V., *Dostoyevsky: The Novel of Discord* (London: Elek, 1976).*

Jones, Malcolm V. and Terry, Garth (eds), *New Essays on Dostoyevsky* (Cambridge: Cambridge University Press, 1983).*

Kaufmann, Walter, *Existentialism from Dostoevsky to Sartre* (Cleveland, Ohio: Meridian, 1956).

Lary, N. M., *Dostoevsky and Dickens* (London and Boston, Mass.: Routledge and Kegan Paul, 1973).

Lawrence, D. H., 'The Grand Inquisitor', in A. Beal (ed.), *Selected Literary Criticism* (London: Mercury, 1961) pp. 233–41.

Linner, Sven, *Starets Zosima in 'The Brothers Karamazov': A Study in the Mimesis of Virtue* (Stockholm: Almqvist and Wiksell, 1975).

Lord, R., *Dostoevsky: Essays and Perspectives* (London: Chatto and Windus, 1970).

Magarshack, David, *Dostoevsky* (London: Secker and Warburg, 1962).

Miller, Robin F., *Dostoevsky and the Idiot: Author, Narrator and Reader* (Cambridge, Mass., and London: Harvard University Press, 1981).

—— (ed.), *Critical Essays on Dostoevsky* (Boston, Mass.: G. K. Hall, 1986).

Mochulsky, Konstantin, *Dostoevsky: His Life and Work*, tr. M. Minihan (Princeton, NJ: Princeton University Press, 1971).

Muchnic, Helen, *Dostoyevsky's English Reputation: 1881–1936* (Northampton, Mass.: Smith College Studies, 1939).

Murry, J. Middleton, *Fyodor Dostoevsky* (London: Martin Secker, 1916).

Nuttall, Anthony D., *'Crime and Punishment': Murder as Philosophic Experiment* (Edinburgh: Sussex University Press, 1978).

Peace, Richard A., *Dostoevsky: An Examination of the Major Novels* (Cambridge: Cambridge University Press, 1971).

Rahv, Philip, *Image and Idea* (New York: New Directions, 1949) pp. 86–110.

Seduro, Vladimir, *Dostoyevski in Russian Literary Criticism 1846–1956* (New York: Octagon Books, 1969).

Shestov, Lev, *Dostoevsky, Tolstoi and Nietzsche* (Athens, Ohio: Ohio University Press, 1969).

Simmons, E. J., *Dostoevsky – The Making of a Novelist* (London: Lehmann, 1950).

Steiner, George, *Tolstoy or Dostoevsky* (London: Faber and Faber, 1959).

Sutherland, Stewart, *Atheism and the Rejection of God: Contemporary Philosophy and the Brothers Karamazov* (Oxford: Basil Blackwell, 1977).

Terras, Victor, *The Young Dostoevsky, 1846–1849: A Critical Study* (The Hague: Mouton, 1969).

Wasiolek, Edward, *Dostoevsky: The Major Fiction* (Cambridge, Mass.: MIT Press, 1964).*

—— (ed.), *'Crime and Punishment' and the Critics* (Belmont, Calif.

——, *The Notebooks for 'Crime and Punishment'* (Chicago and London: University of Chicago Press, 1967).

——, *The Notebooks for 'The Possessed'* (Chicago and London: University of Chicago Press, 1968).

——, *The Notebooks for 'The Idiot'* (Chicago and London: University of Chicago Press, 1969).

——, *The Notebooks for 'The Brothers Karamazov'* (Chicago and London: University of Chicago Press, 1971).

Wellek, René (ed.), *Dostoevsky: A Collection of Critical Essays* (Englewood Cliffs, NJ: Prentice-Hall, 1962).

Wilson, Edmund, 'Dostoevsky Abroad', in *The Shores of Light* (London: W. H. Allen, 1952) pp. 408–14.

Woodhouse, C., *Dostoievski* (London: Barker, 1951).

Index

140